Infection Control
for Body Art

Written by Irene Kennerley

Illustrated by Athena Shultz   Contributions by Alexis Lawson

- Covers OSHA's Bloodborne Pathogens Standard
- Gives samples of important documents, such as an Infection Control Plan for Body Art Professionals
- Covers Exposure Control
- Covers Sharps Disposal
- Standard Precautions
- Practicing Asepsis
- Preventing Cross Contamination in the Workplace

Table of Contents

Preface

It is so important to have complete confidence in our work, and to know that our clients are safe. You may know a lot of the material inside this book--so you're ahead of the game. But as an artist you know that the key to being great is realizing that you can always learn something new.

I wrote this book to help artists like you learn everything you can about infection control, from basic handwashing to creating an effective infection control plan. My wish is that it not only aids you with complying with the law and being safe, but that it also teaches you how and why each practice works. The more informed you are about infection, the better you can work against it.

The first few chapters are a combination of required knowledge, practical knowledge, and fundamentals, such as OSHA's information on hepatitis, how infections are transmitted, and vocabulary such as microorganisms and bloodborne pathogens. Use these chapters as a background and a reference to the following chapters. The next chapters, (4, 5, 6, and 7) outline what to do before, during, and after body art procedures in order to prevent infection. This is the main course of the subject; it can help you pass inspections, keep an attractive workspace, and build confidence in your customers. Chapter 8 is a neat example of some of the paperwork you might need to comply with local regulations. Keep in mind that the forms are written for California state regulations on body art, therefore be sure to modify or create your own to fit your needs.

Most of the research I used comes from textbooks and medical journals, however I found it very important to supplement that knowledge with practical examples as well. Some of the methods described are drawn from dentistry, nursing, and even cosmetology. Government organizations were great resources as well; the CDC, OSHA, FDA, and EPA are great places to start if you ever have a question about hygienic practices or a specific infection.

Of course, if you have questions you can always ask me directly; I want you to know that I am available and welcome questions about infection control in body art. I would love to hear from you.

I come from a body art background in permanent cosmetics, therefore many of the examples and photos you will see in this book are of permanent makeup supplies and practices. However, I wrote this for **all** body art professionals to use, so I encourage you to contact me if you have any other body art photos, (machines, piercing equipment, etc) that you would like to see included in future editions.

In the meantime, enjoy, learn something new, and have fun!

Irene Kennerley

Chapter 1: Infections

Why is This Important?

This book is not about how to cure diseases or how to become a nurse, so why learn about infection? The answer is simple: learning about infectious disease can help you prevent it. The more we know about how infection spreads, the better we can control it when we do body art.

In this book we are going to learn all about infection and how to keep you and your clients safe. Use this book as a guide to your every day routines, and as a reference whenever you have a question about infection. Remember that even the smallest act of prevention can make a difference for your clients.

What is Infection?

Infection is the implantation and reproduction of a disease causing **microorganism** (a tiny, microscopic being invisible to the naked eye, a germ, for example) on top of or inside of the tissues of a **host**. The host can be any living plant, animal, or human being. Sometimes infections

Other words for microorganisms are "microbes" and "germs"

have no symptoms and cause very few effects to their host. Some bacteria are actually beneficial to humans, like those found in yogurt or those that break down waste (more on that later). However, the infections we hear most about are those that show physical signs of illness. When infections cause harmful effects to our bodies we call them **diseases**.

What Causes Disease?

Disease causing microorganisms are called **pathogens**, which means "sickness makers." Pathogens cause disease by damaging tissue or releasing **toxins** (poisons that disrupt bodily functions) into the body of the host.

There are four kinds of pathogens that cause infection:

Viruses

Fungi

Bacteria

Protozoa

Good and Bad Microorganisms: Pathogenic vs. Non-Pathogenic Viruses, Bacteria, Fungi, and Protozoa

Each of the four agents we just discussed are microorganisms, and each one can be **pathogenic** or non-pathogenic. What does this mean?

- **pathogenic microorganisms**, or pathogens, are harmful microorganisms. Think of them as on the **path** to destruction and disease.
- Non-pathogenic **microorganisms** are non-harmful, and even beneficial microorganisms, such as bacteria that break down waste in your stomach.

Here is quick breakdown of which microorganisms are predominantly pathogenic or non-pathogenic:

- Bacteria are mostly non-pathogenic, only a few cause disease

Example: Bacteria are everywhere! There are more than we can count and they cover nearly every surface in nature: food, water, your skin, soil, plants, rocks, trees, you name it!

Bacteria Live on Your Skin

Bacteria Live in Food

Bacteria Live in Nature

- Viruses are mostly **pathogenic**, (disease causing) only a few do not cause disease

Example: The goal of a virus is to invade a host and replicate, which usually kills or damages a living cell. Some helpful viruses actually invade and kill pathogenic bacteria, which truly demonstrates that "The enemy of my enemy is my friend"! An example of a pathogenic virus is HIV.

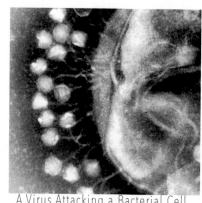

A Virus Attacking a Bacterial Cell

Fungi Like These Mushrooms are Commonly Found in Nature

- Fungi are mostly **non-pathogenic**, only a few cause disease

Example: Fungi, like bacteria, are very common on earth, they exist as yeasts, molds, mushrooms, and much more. An example of a fungal infection is Athlete's Foot

Protozoa Often Live in Water

- Many protozoa (more on them soon!) are **pathogenic**, or disease causing

Example: Protozoa are very animal-like microorganisms, many are commonly found in water. Just like animals, some eat plants, and some eat other animals. When a human is infected by a protozoa, it is being preyed upon. An example of a protozoa infection is malaria.

We are focusing on **pathogenic** microorganisms (pathogens) here, but *remember that not all microorganisms are harmful!*

Vocabulary			
Infection	Pathogens	Fungi	Infectious Agent
Microorganism	Toxins	Protozoa	Microbe
Host	Virus	Pathogenic	Germ
Disease	Bacteria	Non-Pathogenic	

Some Other Things to Remember:

- Just because an infection can hurt a human it doesn't mean that it will hurt (or even be contracted by) plants or animals, and vice versa.

Example: the tulip mosaic virus (seen left) causes beautiful color splashes throughout tulip petals, but causes the flower to die faster than non-infected tulips. This infection cannot be contracted by humans.

The Tulip Mosaic Virus

- A microorganism that is not harmful in or on one part of the human body may become harmful in a different part of the body. For example, Staphylococcus bacteria live on moist areas (your nose, genitals, feet, etc) every day without a problem, but if this same bacteria gets into a cut on your body, you could develop a staph infection. (More on staph infections in Chapter 3.)

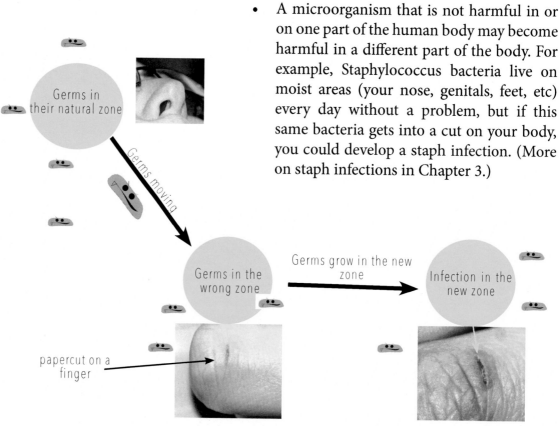

Germs in their natural zone

Germs moving

Germs in the wrong zone

Germs grow in the new zone

Infection in the new zone

papercut on a finger

What is a Germ?

The word **germ** refers to any microorganism, but more specifically to **pathogens** (the sickness makers). When someone avoids the spread of germs, they mean that they avoid spreading any one or all of the four pathogens we just discussed. The word "germ" is often used along with the words "infectious agents," "pathogens," and "microbes." All of these words mean the same thing: a pathogenic, disease causing microorganism.

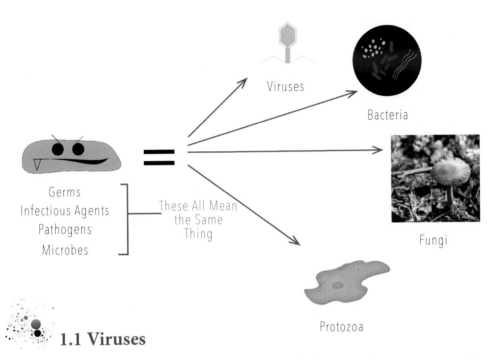

Germs
Infectious Agents
Pathogens
Microbes

These All Mean the Same Thing

Viruses

Bacteria

Fungi

Protozoa

1.1 Viruses

Viruses are the *smallest* of the pathogens and the simplest microorganisms on earth. They contain a tiny core of genetic information, which they inject into a host in order to reproduce, a few proteins, and a protective outer coat which shields them from outside attack. Viruses are so simple, many scientists consider them to just be chemicals, however, they act with so much purpose, many other scientists consider them to be alive!

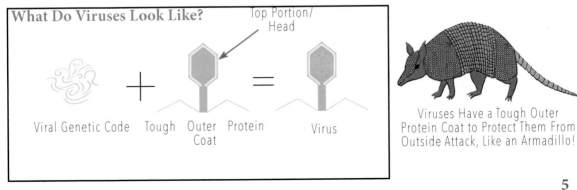

What Do Viruses Look Like?

Top Portion/ Head

Viral Genetic Code   Tough Outer Coat   Protein   Virus

Viruses Have a Tough Outer Protein Coat to Protect Them From Outside Attack, Like an Armadillo!

Viruses invade living cells in the body in order to reproduce. Because the virus lives inside the cell, it is very difficult to destroy. The common cold is a perfect example of viral infection; a tiny pathogen invades the human body through the air or with food, reproduces, and causes your immune system to fight back. The symptoms you feel while you are sick (like coughing, runny nose, and sneezing) are signs that your body is fighting infection.

When Viruses Attack:

Sneezing

Contaminated Food

Kissing and Contact with Infected People

Why Do We Sneeze?

We sneeze when our noses/sinuses are stimulated, meaning that something foreign such as light, bacteria, or even a needle has disturbed the nerves that control our sinuses. A piece of debris, such as pepper, can stimulate your nerves and cause the muscles in your chest to contract very quickly, forcing air, mucus, and saliva across a room at about 100 miles per hour! Sneezing removes and cleans out your nose in order to better protect against pathogens. However, remember that if you do not cover your nose and mouth when you sneeze, you have just launched potentially sickness causing germs across a room. If other people are across the room, you may have transmitted pathogens through the air straight at them! Always cover your mouth and nose when coughing or sneezing, and stay home from work if you are sick until you feel better.

Virus Example	If you have ever had cold sores in your life, you carry the herpes simplex type 1 virus(HSV-1). 90% of people worldwide have this virus and most people don't realize they have it, many show no symptoms. Herpes simplex type 1 causes sores on the mouth and lips. It is spread by contact with an infected person's cold sores, via acts such as kissing, sharing a lipstick (or trying one on at a makeup counter that an infected person also tried on), or even sharing a drink. **Why is this important?** Clients who develop cold sores on their lips after a lip procedure can lose 90% of the implanted color in that area. To avoid this, clients with HSV-1 need to take a preventative medication (such as Valtrex®) before having their lips done to ensure that cold sores don't develop.

Some Examples of Diseases Caused By Viruses

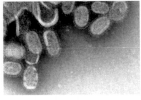

Influenza

AIDS

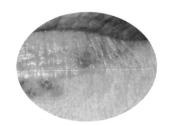

Herpes Virus

Not all viruses make you feel sick, because they often choose a specific tissue to reproduce in, such as the mouth, respiratory tract, or sexual organs. The tissue affected depends on the specific virus infecting the body.

Some viruses such as the common cold and the flu can be completely overcome by the body, while others cannot. Some examples of viruses that cannot be completely overcome are Hepatitis B, AIDS, and herpes.

The Difference Between a Common Cold and the Flu:

As you may have seen firsthand, the common cold and the flu are very similar. You can cough, sneeze, have a sore throat, and feel weak with both, however there are very few symptoms that can help you tell them apart. The flu is usually a faster infection, meaning you can go from feeling great to feeling awful within hours, versus a cold may take a few days to develop. A flu is usually accompanied by a fever, whereas a cold usually is not. There are a few other subtle differences, such as a runny nose is usually a cold symptom, and coughs are usually a flu symptom. Infections often have a unique set of symptoms (coughing, sneezing, etc) that help doctors identify what a sick person might have. While some may be easy to tell apart, other infections are harder and could require tests.

What Kind of Infection Do I Have?

When it comes to knowing if you have a particular type of infection (bacterial, viral, fungal, etc) the symptoms for infection are so varied it can be difficult to tell! Pathogens are extremely different on a microscopic level, but the effects they produce on the body are often very similar! Coughing, runny nose, and fever could all be symptoms of infection by viruses, bacteria, fungi, or protozoa. All in all, you can't really tell which one you have until it develops unique symptoms, such as vomiting with the flu or a painful sore throat with strep throat (bacterial infection).

Killing Viruses:

To kill viruses in the environment, we sterilize tools and disinfect surfaces with chemicals strong enough to destroy a virus's protective coat. Chemical disinfectants that can kill viruses are said to be **virucidal**.

You can also prevent the spread of viruses by covering coughs and sneezes, and washing your hands after doing so.

Ball Shaped

Rod Shaped

Spiral Shaped

1.2 Bacteria

Bacteria are single-celled microorganisms that like to live in tissues (such as the soft lining of your stomach), rather than in other living cells.

There are three main shapes of bacteria: the ball shaped **cocci**, (pronounced "cock-eye"), the rod shaped **bacilli** (pronounced "botch-ill-eye"), and a spiral shape called **spirilla** (pronounced "spur-ill-ah").

Bacteria are living organisms

These shapes and names are important because they help us identify bacteria. Most of these names come from Greek and Latin roots. For example, *Staphylococcus* (pronounced "staff-ah-low-kah-kus") bacteria lets us know that these are ball shaped bacteria, and they belong to the **cocci** family. The word coccus stems from the Greek word *kokkos*, meaning seed.

The "Staphylo" part is a prefix that lets us separate it from other bacteria by naming a unique quality, such as how the bacteria clusters together, or how it moves in the body.

Now, you don't need to know how bacteria move, but it is helpful to know where these names come from.

Bacteria have a variety of functions, and *most of them are not bad!* Less than 1% of all bacteria cause disease. Most do not affect you at all, and many bacteria are even helpful! Humans often put bacteria to work to solve a specific problem or serve specific purposes, such as making pickles out of cucumbers. Bacteria are used to make cheese, yogurt, vinegar, buttermilk, sour cream, sauerkraut, and much more.

✖
Pathogenic bacteria are harmful

✔
Non-pathogenic bacteria are non-harmful

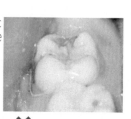

✖ Tooth Decay

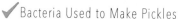

✔ Bacteria Used to Make Pickles

✔ Yogurt Bacteria

Bacteria in Recycling: Why Does Garbage Smell?

In recycling, bacteria are used to break down waste, such as sewage, garbage, and chemicals. Bacteria eat garbage, which makes it smell. The smell of rotting food is a sure sign that bacteria are eating it and breaking it down into simple liquids and gases. This process is called **decomposition**. The liquids and gases given off during decomposition create the unique stink of garbage.

Decomposition

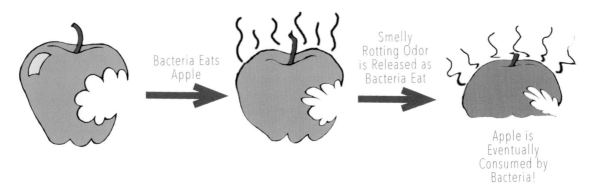

Bacteria Eats Apple

Smelly Rotting Odor is Released as Bacteria Eat

Apple is Eventually Consumed by Bacteria!

Bacteria in Food: How is Yogurt Made? Why is it OK to Eat?

Yogurt is made by mixing certain bacteria into milk, where it *ferments* and produces yogurt's signature acidic/tangy taste. **Fermentation** is the process by which we make microorganisms (such as fungi and bacteria) partially eat food and change its qualities, whether that be taste, smell, cooking time, or nutrition. Once a certain bacterium has been mixed into milk, it eats the milk's proteins to produce lactic acid, which gives yogurt its tang! Special care is taken so that only non-harmful microorganisms can grow during fermentation, this is why yogurt is safe to eat. Lactic acid is actually very good for you, and so are the **probiotic bacteria** that live in your yogurt!

Fermentation

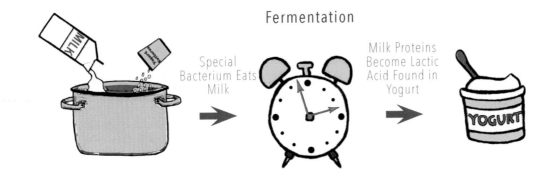

Special Bacterium Eats Milk

Milk Proteins Become Lactic Acid Found in Yogurt

YOGURT

In the Human Body

In the human body, there are actually 10 times more bacteria living in and on your body than human body cells! Bacteria are very small, so they take up less space than most human cells. Their small size and large numbers mean they live all around you, and inside of you! Bacteria in the body help you digest food, combat harmful pathogens on your skin, and even boost your immune system. Bacteria that are good for your body are called **probiotic bacteria**.

Pathogenic Bacteria

Harmful, **pathogenic bacteria** cause disease, such as tooth decay and tuberculosis. They enter the body through the air, through contaminated food, insect bites, sexual contact, and wounds. Once inside, grow until they reach nearly double their original size, and then divide into two new daughter cells. This reproductive process is called **binary fission**.

Under ideal conditions, a few bacteria can multiply to millions within hours, damaging surrounding tissue and/or releasing toxins that cause disease. Bacterial toxins are responsible for the effects of tetanus, some food poisoning, and blood poisoning (bacteria in the blood which causes infection).

Bacteria Entering the Human Body

Bacteria can enter the body through...

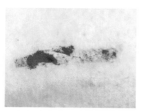

A Cut or Scrape

Eating Rotting Fruit or Meat

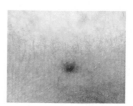

An Insect Bite

Most infections enter through the same routes: wounds, sexual contact, contaminated food/water, and contaminated objects/people. Bacteria can be destroyed many different ways. Most bacteria cannot resist heat for a long period of time, which is why we cook raw foods before eating.

In the workplace, we can kill bacteria with chemical disinfectants and sterilization. Disinfectants are enough to kill bacteria, but not their **spores**. More on spores in a moment! A disinfectant that has the ability to kill fully grown bacteria is said to be **bactericidal**.

Your Body's Natural Defenses

If pathogens do successfully invade the body (via a cut, passing a cold, etc), your white blood cells react by making very special molecules called **antibodies. Antibodies** are proteins that help destroy pathogens. They do this by finding and locking onto signals from pathogens called **antigens. Antigens** are chemical signals from pathogens that our bodies use to find and destroy them. Once antibodies have found and locked onto the antigens, other immune cells arrive and destroy them.

Once your body has been exposed to a pathogen, your immune system remembers how to produce the unique antibodies that would lock onto that pathogen. This special way of remembering how to protect you from pathogens is called **immunity**.

Antibody molecules are Y-shaped

10

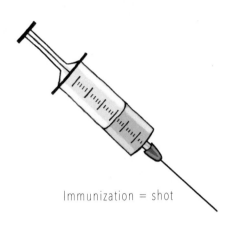

Immunization = shot

In addition to disinfection and sterilization, many bacterial infections can be prevented with **vaccines**, which give **immunity** to the vaccinated person for that disease. This is why we call shots and vaccines **immunizations, or vaccinations**.

Vaccines work two ways. The first way is that you get a shot of a very weak form of the disease you are trying to avoid. This helps your body learn and remember how to make antibodies for that disease. This kind of immunity is called **active immunity**. Active immunity is usually permanent. The second way is to get a shot with antibodies that can kill the disease you are trying to avoid. These antibodies often come from another animal that has developed immunity. Receiving antibodies from another organism is called passive immunity. Passive immunity is temporary, because your body will eventually destroy any foreign antibodies from other sources. Mother's milk is a great example of this. When a mother breastfeeds, her antibodies are passed to her child, who becomes temporarily immune to many infectious diseases. This helps the child defend itself against pathogens until its immune system begins to produce its own antibodies, which begins a few months after birth.

Note!

Body art is not recommended for pregnant or nursing mothers. Why? Because any infection/ complication can be easily spread to the fetus during pregancy, or spread to a child during nursing

Treating Bacterial Infections: Antibiotics

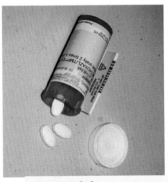

Sometimes your immune system and natural antibodies are not enough to fight infection. If you are already sick with a bacterial infection, you can take **antibiotics**, which either kill or prevent the growth and reproduction of bacteria, depending on the drug. Certain antibiotics are effective against fungi, protozoa, and bacteria, but none are effective against viruses.

Vocabulary		
Virucidal	Decomposition	Binary Fission
Antigens	Cocci	Fermentation
Spores	Immunity	Bacilli
Probiotic Bacteria	Bactericidal	Vaccine/Vaccination
Pathogenic Bacteria	Antibodies	Immunization
Spirilla	Active Immunity	Antibiotics

11

Alexander Fleming discovered penicillin in 1928

The discovery of antibiotics changed the world! In 1928, Alexander Fleming accidentally discovered penicillin when one of his experiments was contaminated with a strange mold. He discovered that this mold was not only safe for humans, but it inhibited the growth of many different kinds of bacteria. As a result of his invention, deadly diseases such as pneumonia have become much less of a threat now than they were in the 1930s. There are at least 20 different kinds of penicillin in use today to treat bacterial infections ranging from simple throat infections to certain sexually transmitted diseases (STDs).

Dangers of Antibiotics and Antibiotic Resistance

Antibiotics are wonderful for particularly nasty infections that won't go away, but you shouldn't take them for every infection you get. They are widely regarded as safe, but here are some of the dangers of antibiotics:

- Many antibiotics will kill both pathogenic and non-pathogenic bacteria in the area for which you take them (stomach, throat, etc). If too many non-pathogenic bacteria are killed, pathogenic bacteria can outcompete them for food, causing a much worse infection that could need more complicated drugs.
- Many people are allergic to antibiotics, just taking them could cause unpleasant side effects such as rash, diarrhea, or fever. In rare cases, some people are so severely allergic that antibiotics could end their life.
- Very rarely, antibiotics can cause tissue damage by killing human body cells as they target harmful cells. One example of this is silver. Using silver as an antibiotic can allow heavy metals into internal organs, where they can cause accumulate and cause disfunction.
- Antibiotics kill all of the weaker strains of bacteria in the affected area, meaning only the strongest survive and reproduce. If only strong bacteria live in your body, antibiotics will no longer work. Bacteria can grow resistant to antibiotics over time. This is called **antibiotic resistance**.

Antibiotic Resistance

Antibiotic resistance is a major problem, because bacteria are beginning to evolve faster than we can create new antibiotics to fight them. New "superbugs" are mutating from the offspring of the few strains that survive treatment with antibiotics. A very serious (and relevant!) example of this is a staph infection, which is a skin infection commonly caused by bacteria entering an open wound such as a tattoo. We will talk more about staph infections in Chapter 3.

Staph infections used to be treated with methicillin (a type of penicillin), but over time this infection became resistant, and the new bacteria was named *Methicillin-resistant Staphylococcus aureus,* or MRSA. (More in Chapter 3)

12

Spores

Bacteria with extra protective layers are called **spores (or *endospores*)**. Bacteria form spores when food is scarce or when conditions become extremely harsh. An extra protective coating of tough protein helps spores resist extreme heat, cold, and environmental damage. Because of this tough extra coating, spores cannot be destroyed by normal disinfection; they can live for years until conditions become favorable again. Spores will only die when exposed to extreme heat and pressure, such as those produced by an autoclave. This is why we sterilize objects used in the workplace. If spores are not destroyed, (in other words, if you do not sterilize your tweezers and other implements) they may live on, reproduce, and become ready to infect a human being.

Adding Layers of Protection

Bacteria   Bacterial Spore (Endospore)

What Does it Take to Kill a Spore?

Spores have a protective layer of rigid protein in cells that helps them resist damage from the outside world. In order to kill spores and prevent the spread of infection from bacteria, you must **sterilize** your reusable objects with enough **time, heat,** and **pressure** to destroy a spore's protective coating. **Sterilization means to destroy all microorganisms and their spores on an object.** You can use an autoclave, a dry heat sterilizer, a chemical vapor system, or an ethylene oxide machine to sterilize used items.

Three criteria needed to kill spores:
Time: Time needed to kill
Heat: Temperature needed to kill
Pressure: Weight/force needed to kill

How Much Heat/Pressure is Enough?	
Autoclaves:	250-270°F and 15-30 psi
Dry Heat:	250-340°F (Temperatures close to 250°F require longer cycle time)
Chemical Vapor:	270°F and 20 psi
Ethylene Oxide:	86-140°F (the gas does the rest of the work)

***Time needed to kill may depend on the sterilizer brand and implements used

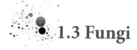

1.3 Fungi

Fungi are yeasts and molds, such as the yeast that bread is baked with, mold on blue cheese, and mushrooms. Most fungi are harmless, and some are even beneficial.

The Fungus Among Us: Fungi in Nature

Mushrooms

Fungi often feed on dead matter, such as rotting trees and fruit. The mold that you see growing on rotting fruit is actually a fungus eating the fruit. There are many different kinds of fungi, some eat dead organisms, some feed on live organisms, and some live in an interesting partnership with other living things. For example, certain fungi grow and live with orchids to help them spread their seeds. Orchid seeds lack the nutrients needed to sprout, but fungi can exchange some of their own until the orchid is old enough to exchange food back with them.

Fungi in Food

Many fungi are edible (like mushrooms), or help create other edible things, such as bread, cheese, and wine. In one step of the winemaking process, yeast, (a form of fungi) is mixed with mashed grapes or grape juice and allowed to eat the grapes' natural sugars. The yeast converts the sugars into alcohol and carbon dioxide gas, which is released into the atmosphere.

In breadmaking, the release of carbon dioxide gas causes dough to rise. Yeast is added to the dough, eats the sugar inside, and produces alcohol and carbon dioxide. The gas pushes the dough out from the inside, making it rise up. When the bread is baked, the alcohol is burned off, leaving a nice, fluffy loaf of bread!

Do you see a pattern here? Yes! These foods are all produced by **fermentation**, where the action of a living organism is used to create a product. The only difference between bacterial fermentation and fungal fermentation is that here a fungus is doing the fermenting instead of bacteria.

Blue Cheese is Made With a Special Type of Mold to Give a Distinct Flavor

Disease Causing Fungi

Some fungi can cause disease by multiplying and spreading on the human body. Fungal infections are usually skin or nail related. Diseases caused by fungi are often characterized by red, itchy, and/or flaky skin. Some examples of fungal infections are athlete's foot, ringworm, and nail fungus.

Fungi on the Human Body

Sharing a hat with a ringworm patient

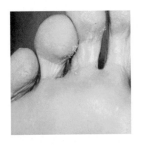

Athlete's Foot

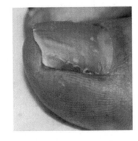

Nail Fungus

Prevention and Treatment of Fungal Infections

Fungi like to grow in warm, moist places—such as the webbing between toes in the case of Athlete's Foot. The easiest way to prevent fungal infections is good personal hygiene. Keep any affected moist areas clean and dry, and change personal garments such as socks regularly. Maintaining a clean, dry area for yourself prevents fungi from growing. Fungal infections can sometimes be treated with antibiotics, but other times they require special antifungal medications to go away. In the case of yeast infections, an antifungal medication called fluconazole ("floo-con-ah-zole") is used to target the yeast and stop its growth. A yeast infection is an overgrowth of *Candida* fungus in the vagina. This imbalance causes redness, itching, and abnormal discharge.

Most of the treatments for these infections are over-the-counter powders and ointments, but sometimes stronger infections require prescription drugs to treat.

Fungal Spores vs. Bacterial Spores

Fungi also create spores when they reproduce. Fungal spores are different from bacterial spores: Fungal spores are created as fungi reproduce, and bacterial spores are created when outside conditions become harsh. The types of spores are similar, however; the spores of fungi are tough like those of bacteria, the only way to kill them is with sterilization.

Fungal Spores

1.4 Protozoa

Protozoa are living organisms

Protozoa are a lot like microscopic animals! Another name you might know protozoa by is the amoeba ("ah-mee-bah"), a single celled animal that lives in stagnant water. Amoebas can live in the bloodstream, the intestines, and the mouth. These animals reproduce by changing shape and then dividing in half. It is rare to become seriously ill from protozoa in the United States; it is more common in countries where water is extremely polluted. Some examples of diseases caused by protozoa are malaria, amoebic dysentery, and trichomoniasis. Trichomoniasis, or "trich" for short, is the most common curable **sexually transmitted disease (STD)** in the United States. Trich is caused by a microscopic parasite in the genital area, and gives symptoms of itching, burning, and abnormal discharge.

Amoebic dysentery is a bowel infection caused by eating or drinking something that has a pathogenic amoeba living in it. The amoeba causes weight loss, dehydration, and diarrhea, but is easily treated with antibiotics.

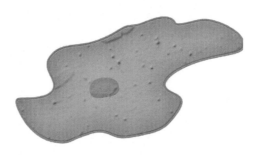

Amoeba

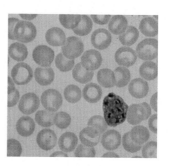

Malaria

Malaria is a very serious disease spread in tropical regions by mosquitos. The specific pathogen that causes the disease lives in the saliva of infected female mosquitos. When an infected female bites a human, the protozoa is transferred directly to the bloodstream, then to the liver, where it grows and multiplies. Malaria is difficult for the human immune system to attack because once inside the liver this pathogen disguises itself with liver cells. Antibodies only "see" normal human cells, no pathogens. From here the parasites infect red blood cells, causing fever, flu-like symptoms, and even death.

Vector transmission is the reason animals (besides service animals) are not allowed in work areas

Diseases spread by animals are important to learn about because keeping clean environments can help us avoid them. Infected animals, people, or other living things that spread and carry disease are called **vectors**. Mosquitos, ticks, and fleas contaminate objects and people by landing on them, biting, eating, and defecating. You can prevent vector transmitted diseases by maintaining a clean environment separate from food areas, living spaces, and pet areas.

Types of Infection

All of the pathogens we just discussed have the potential to cause disease, but under what circumstances? Some pathogens attack the body when it is weak, some when it is strong, and some when we are in the hospital. The way a pathogen attacks helps us classify how infection happens and how to help prevent it.

Endogenous Infection

This is an infection or disease that comes from **within** the body and does not transmit to other people. Examples are diseases that are usually dormant that flare up from time to time, such as yeast infections or urinary tract infections.

Exogenous Infection

This type of infection comes from **outside** the body, through the chain of infection. Examples include the common cold and the flu, which you can get from other people or from your environment.

Nosocomial Infection (pronounced "noss"-"oh"-"koh"-"mial")

Also called Hospital Acquired infections, Nosocomial infections happen in **hospitals**. These infections may be endogenous or exogenous, meaning they can come up from within the body as an underlying (incubating) infection such as HIV, or they can come from outside the body via cross contamination, such as a cold. Pathogens cross over from hospital workers who do not wash their hands properly, forget to change their gloves, or use contaminated equipment.

One example of a nosocomial infection is Hospital Acquired Pneumonia (HAP). Pneumonia bacteria from one patient can travel through the air and can infect the lungs of other patients. This can happen with contaminated equipment such as mechanical ventilators (for helping patients breathe), from hospital workers who do not wash their hands, or simply from the air in the hospital. If the air in the hospital is not filtered or exchanged enough to remove the bacteria, it can be spread very easily to others.

Hospital
Acquired
Pneumonia
(HAP)

Types of Infection

Opportunistic Infection

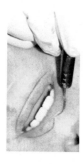

Opportunistic infections occur when a pathogen has a special *opportunity* to attack. This can be when the body's immune system is weakened and cannot effectively resist disease, or if bacteria multiply in a place they shouldn't. Some examples of opportunistic infections are tuberculosis and herpes simplex type 1. Tuberculosis remains dormant in the body, but flares up from time to time. Herpes (cold sores) breakouts occur when lips experience trauma, such as a permanent lip procedure or lip piercing.

- Opportunistic infections can happen in anyone, however the rate of infection is much higher in people with weakened immune systems, such as AIDS patients.
- **Opportunistic infections can also be any of the other types we just talked about: Endogenous, Exogenous, or Hospital Acquired/Nosocomial**

Example 1:

- A urinary tract infection can be opportunistic and endogenous. (It actually can be hospital acquired too!) The infection comes from *inside* the body when bacteria from the intestines (where food is digested) gets into the urinary tract (or bladder) and uses that *opportunity* to multiply there.

Example 2:

- A staph infection (more on staph infections in Chapter 3) on a tattoo can be both opportunistic and exogenous. It is opportunistic because the skin on the tattoo is open to any staph bacteria from the environment. Staph bacteria can be from the client's own skin or from cross contamination with contaminated objects. This is why it is so important to have your clients follow post treatment instructions, because they can easily infect themselves!

Example 2:

- Hospital Acquired Pneumonia (HAP) can be opportunistic, exogenous, *and* nosocomial. If a sick person with an already weakened immune system goes to the hospital and gets HAP from the air, they would have an infection that was from outside the body, from a hospital, and was opportunistic, since they already had a weakened immune system!

Chapter 1 Vocabulary:

Infection · Pathogens · Fungi · Infectious Agent
Microorganism · Toxins · Protozoa · Microbe
Host · Virus · Pathogenic · Germ
Disease · Bacteria · Non-Pathogenic · Sterilization
Virucidal · Decomposition · Binary Fission · Antigens
Cocci · Fermentation · Spores · Immunity
Bacilli · Probiotic Bacteria · Bactericidal · Vaccine
Spirilla · Pathogenic Bacteria · Antibodies · Vaccination
Active Immunity · Antibiotics · Antibiotic Resistance · Immunization
Sexually Transmitted Disease (STD) · Malaria · Vector
Endogenous Infection · Exogenous Infection
Nosocomial/Hospital Acquired Infection · Opportunistic Infection

Chapter 1: Test Your Knowledge Questions

2. What are the four types of pathogens?

3. Name the three shapes of bacteria.

4. True or False: All viruses can be cured. If false, give an example of an incurable virus.

5. What is a toxin?

6. True or False: All bacteria are bad.

7. Why can't bacterial spores (endospores) be destroyed by normal disinfection?

    a. Superpowers
    b. They are too small
    c. They have an extra coating
    d. None of the above

8. How can you destroy bacterial spores?

9. Where do fungi like to grow?

    a. In the forest
    b. Warm, moist places
    c. Cool, dry places
    d. None of the above

10. What are protozoa?

11. How is Malaria spread? What do we call this kind of transmission?

12. What is the difference between fungal spores and bacterial spores?

13. What is sterilization?

14. What temperatures and pressures are needed for sterilization to happen (Name for any kind of sterilization)?

15. What is antibiotic resistance?

16. Who discovered penicillin?

17. What kind of bacteria are used to make yogurt?

    a. Non-pathogenic bacteria
    b. Probiotic bacteria
    c. Living bacteria
    d. All of the above

18. Based on where fungi like to grow, (see your answer to number 9) how can you prevent them from growing? What kind of environment should you create?

19. What is a vector for disease?

20. Name the 4 types of infection.

21. Hospital Acquired Pneumonia is 3 of the 4 types of infection all at once! Explain how this can happen.

Chapter 1: Bonus Crossword

Across

7. Medicine that kills or prevents the growth and reproduction of bacteria when your body is unable to fight the infection itself

10. A pathogen that invades living cells in order to reproduce and cause infection; smallest and simplest microorganisms

11. When your body is able to remember how to protect you from pathogens

13. An infection that emerges from outside the body

14. Also known as vaccines

16. Any microorganism that causes illness

19. The process of receiving a vaccine to build immunity

22. Non-harmful bacteria

24. The offspring of a bacterium with extra protective layers

27. An infection that emerges from inside the body

29. A form of bacteria, fungi, a virus, or protozoa that can potentially infect a host; the first link in the chain of infection

31. Disease that is spread through sexual contact

35. Also known as immunizations

36. Chemical signals from pathogens that our bodies use to find and destroy them

39. An infection contracted in a hospital

40. Harmful, disease causing bacteria

Down

1. Bacteria that is good for you: bacteria in yogurt
2. The process of killing bacteria and their spores using heat, pressure, and/or chemicals
3. A tiny, microscopic being that is invisible to the naked eye
4. The implantation and reproduction of a disease causing microorganism
5. Also known as an amoeba, a microscopic animal that lives in water
6. Ball shaped bacteria
7. A usually permanent type of immunity
8. Process of microorganisms partially eating food and changing its qualities
9. Harmful microorganisms that are the path to destruction and disease
12. Yeasts and molds that often feed on dead matter
15. Rod shaped bacteria
17. A microscopic organism
18. Disease causing microorganisms/sickness makers
19. Infected animals, people, or other living things that spread and carry diseases
20. When the strongest bacteria are not completely killed with treatment and reproduce to make "superbugs" that available medicine is unable to destroy
21. Single-celled microorganisms that like to live in tissues
23. Infections that are harmful to our bodies
25. Any living plant, animal, or human being
26. Bacteria killing
28. Virus killing
30. When bacteria break down an organism into simple liquids and gases
32. Poisons that disrupt bodily functions
33. Spiral shaped bacteria
34. Proteins made by white blood cells that help destroy pathogens
37. Amoebic disease spread by mosquitos in tropical regions
38. Reproductive process of bacteria
41. An infection that takes advantage of a body in a weakened state

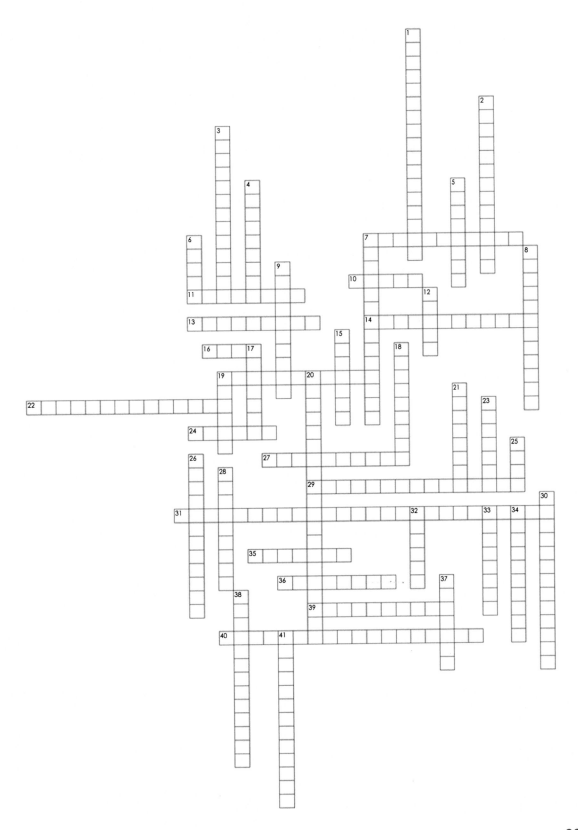

23

Notes

Notes

Chapter 2: How Does Disease Spread?

Learning Objectives for This Chapter:

- Understand the Chain of Infection
- Be able to give examples of each component in the chain of infection
- Be able to give examples of how to cut the chain of infection at each component
- Understand the importance or preventing cross contamination
- Know what OPIM is and be able to identify the most likely OPIM that you would encounter in the workplace
- Know the characteristics of the five stages of infection

How do germs travel and infect people? Every disease is different, but in general pathogens follow a chain of events called "**The Chain of Infection.**" Germs, or "Infectious Agents," need a home to start with and breed in (reservoir), a way to leave their home (portal of exit), and a way to travel to and enter a new host(means of transmission and portal of entry). Completing the chain causes infection, but **breaking the chain at any point can prevent infection**.

 2.1 The Chain of Infection

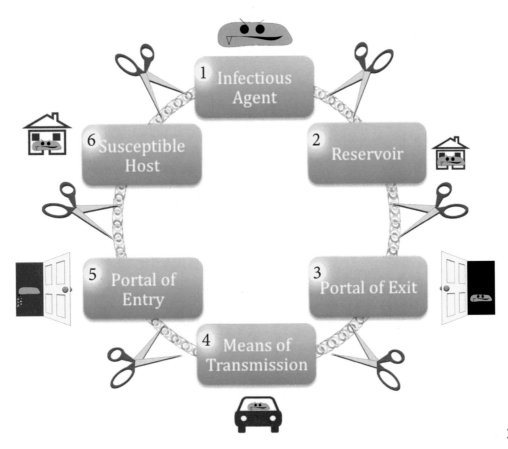

1 The Infectious Agent: The Germ

Infection starts with an **infectious agent**. This agent is a harmful, disease causing pathogen. It can be a virus, bacteria, fungus, or protozoa.

Cut the Chain!

Removing germs with handwashing

You can remove and kill germs several ways:

- Wash your hands to remove germs
- Disinfect surfaces to kill germs
- Sterilize your implements to kill germs

Maintaining good hygiene, preventing cross contamination, and keeping your workplace clean can cut the Chain of Infection at any step.

2 The Reservoir: Where Germs Live

A reservoir is the place where germs comes from. This is a pathogen's home. A reservoir can be any of the following:

- An infected person (vector)

- A person with poor hygiene (vector)

- Contaminated equipment (such as dirty machines)

- Dirty floors and walls

- Dirty clothing

- Contaminated food

- Contaminated water

- Animals (vector)

- Insects (vector)

- Dirty gloves

- Spills that have not been cleaned up

- Sinks with food or dirty dishes inside

Pets harbor germs in their fur

Cut the Chain!

You can prevent a germ's reservoir by:

- Staying at home when you are sick

- Practicing proper hygiene

- Cleaning, disinfecting, and/or sterilizing your equipment properly

- Cleaning your floors, walls, counters, and other surfaces regularly with disinfectant

- Always changing your labcoat and gloves when they get dirty, and between every client

- Keeping food, water, and pets away from your work area

- Not smoking in your work area

- Keeping your kitchen areas separate from your work area (no food or food dishes in sinks where you wash your hands)

- Cleaning up spills immediately

Cleaning up spills as they happen

Disinfecting surfaces

Handwashing is the easiest and most effective way to prevent infection

Transient and Resident Germs

The human body is an incredible reservoir for pathogens. There are two kinds of microbes present all over the body: transient and resident.

The word _transient_ means _impermanent_ or _temporary_. Transient microbes are germs loosely attached to our skin from normal daily activities. This kind of microbe is easily removed with proper handwashing.

Transient germs are easily gained with daily activities

Transient germs are easily removed with handwashing

Resident microbes are **residents** of our bodies, and live deep in the tiny cracks and crevices of our skin. Everyone's resident bacteria is different, and is influenced by the environment they are in. For example, a teacher will have different resident germs on her skin than a dentist or medical professional. These microbes are very difficult to remove, but most can be removed with proper handwashing, which uses friction to get inside some of these deep crevices.

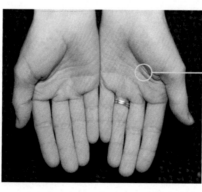

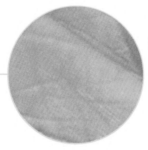

Resident bacteria live in the tiny cracks and crevices of our skin

Skin with a lot of hair on it (your head, underarms, etc) harbors pathogens which can be spread to others very easily. While they may be harmless to you, they can cause another person to get sick. Keep long hair tied back and/or covered, practice good personal hygiene, and wash your hands properly to help prevent the spread of germs.

Germm Hotspots

The human body is home to thousands of different microorganisms, mostly bacteria. There are some fungi and even a few parasites too!

Warm, moist places and areas with sweat and oil (also called *sebaceous*) glands make it easy for bacteria and fungi to grow.

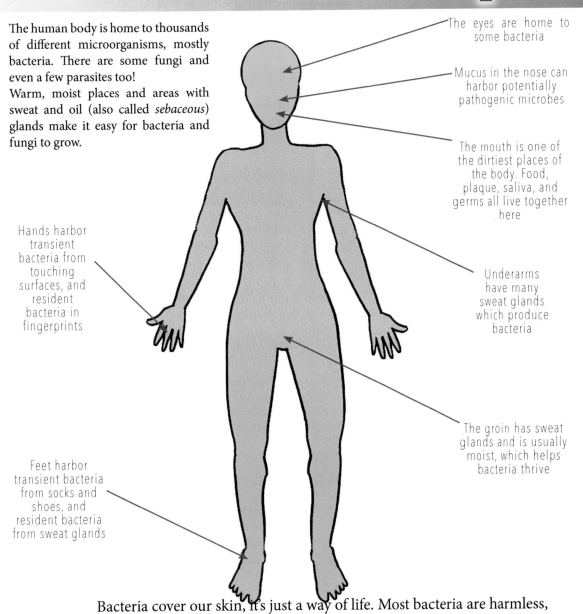

The eyes are home to some bacteria

Mucus in the nose can harbor potentially pathogenic microbes

The mouth is one of the dirtiest places of the body. Food, plaque, saliva, and germs all live together here

Underarms have many sweat glands which produce bacteria

The groin has sweat glands and is usually moist, which helps bacteria thrive

Hands harbor transient bacteria from touching surfaces, and resident bacteria in fingerprints

Feet harbor transient bacteria from socks and shoes, and resident bacteria from sweat glands

An antiseptic is a disinfectant or antimicrobial agent applied to the skin to prevent infection

Bacteria cover our skin, it's just a way of life. Most bacteria are harmless, however just because they are harmless to you does not mean they cannot hurt someone else. Washing your hands before every procedure is mandatory to keep your own personal bacteria away from your clients. A client's own bacteria can cause infection as well! The act of a needle going into the skin can push bacteria inside, causing infection at the site of the procedure. You must always remember to cleanse your client's skin with an **antiseptic** such as an alcohol wipe, or antimicrobial soap and water before working to prevent the spread of germs.

3 The Portal of Exit: The Open Door

The portal of exit is the pathogen's door from its reservoir to the outside world. A portal of exit can be a sneeze, cough, wound/cut, or secretion of bodily fluids such as blood or saliva.

Cut the Chain!

Covering a cough can prevent pathogens from being carried through the air

You can prevent a portal of exit for germs by:

- Staying at home when you are sick

- Covering your mouth when you cough or sneeze

- Bandaging cuts

- Keeping your nose and mouth covered while you work (using a face mask)

4 Means of Transmission: Travel Through Contaminated Objects

Once the pathogen has left the reservoir, it needs a way to spread to a new host. Germs can **cross over** from contaminated objects to clean ones with the touch of a dirty glove or an unclean implement; this accidental spread of germs is called **cross contamination**. Here are some ways infectious agents are transported:

- Through contact with contaminated objects (cross contamination)

- Through contact with the eyes, nose, or mouth

- Through the air

- Through blood and open wounds

- Through contaminated food/water

- Through contaminated people, pets, or insects (vectors)

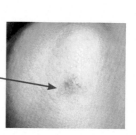

Open wounds are always at risk for infection

Cut the Chain! ✂

You can prevent a means of transmission/cross contamination by:

- Changing your gloves when they get dirty

- Keeping your nose and mouth covered while you work (wearing a face mask)

- Using barriers (such as treatment bed paper and barrier film) to prevent contamination of clean surfaces

- Using only sterile equipment and as many disposable, single use items as possible

- Many other ways, which we will discuss later!

5 The Portal of Entry: A Way Inside

An infectious agent needs a doorway to enter a new home and infect a susceptible person. Common ways pathogens enter the human body are through broken skin (from a finished procedure or a needle stick) and mucous membranes (your eyes, nose, and mouth). Any opening in the body is a target for infectious agents; this is why clients must take extra care to keep their finished procedures clean.

Cut the Chain! ✂

You can prevent a portal of entry by:

Open wounds such as new tattoos can be a portal of entry for pathogens

- Covering your nose and mouth with a face mask while you work

- Wearing goggles or eye shields to protect your eyes while you work

- Keeping any cuts bandaged/isolated from germs

- Making sure clients keep their procedures clean as they heal

6 Susceptible Host

This is the last link in the chain of infection. A susceptible host is a new person or animal that cannot resist the transmitted pathogen and becomes infected. This host becomes a new **reservoir** for the pathogen, and the chain starts all over again.

Think of the susceptible host as the hostess of a party with many guests. She opens her front door so that invited guests can come in and out of the house, but while the door is open, a few party crashers slip inside. Before the hostess knows it, her party is full of loud, violent, and obnoxious party crashers!

The hostess needs to call the police to remove the bad guests to get her house back, the same way your body needs to call on it's immune system to fight invading pathogens.

Cut the Chain!

You can prevent a susceptible host from getting sick by:

- Taking good care of your personal health to provide resistance to pathogens

- Practicing good personal hygiene to prevent excess exposure to germs

- Keeping new tattoos and piercings clean

- Avoiding sick people and contaminated items, surfaces, and animals

- Avoiding healthy people if you are sick

- Avoiding working on clients with weakened immune systems, unless a doctor gives permission

34

The Five Stages of Infection

The Incubation Stage

Once a pathogen has completed the chain of infection and entered a new host, a period of time passes before the infected person begins to show symptoms. This period of time is called the incubation stage, and can range from a few minutes to many years, depending on the pathogen. HIV is an example of a pathogen that may incubate in the body for many years.

The Prodromal Stage

This is when symptoms of disease first occur. These symptoms are usually not specific to any disease yet; they are simply the body's natural response to infection. The infected person may experience headache, nausea, vomiting, fever, rash, or diarrhea.

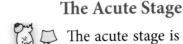

The Acute Stage

The acute stage is the peak of infection. At this point, symptoms have fully developed and become unique to the pathogen causing disease. An example of this is when a person with strep throat suddenly develops the throat pain that lets them know they have strep throat.

The Declining Stage

At this stage the infected person begins to feel better. The infection is still present, however the symptoms begin to subside.

The Convalescent Stage

"Convalescence" means "healing". This is the last stage of infection. The body finishes fighting disease-causing pathogens and begins to recover. The infected person returns to normal.

How Long Should I Stay Home When I'm Sick?

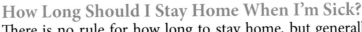

There is no rule for how long to stay home, but generally people stay home until the Acute stage of the infection is over and they feel better. Usually the time you are most contagious is at the beginning of an infection. The risk of infection decreases as you begin to heal. Some infections can still be spread to others even after a week or two after you have had them, so always use caution and wash your hands to prevent the spread of germs.

2.2 How Bloodborne Pathogens Affect Body Artists: Exposure Determination and Risks

"Exposure Determination" is an OSHA term that means to **determine** the tasks in body art that could lead to **exposure** to bloodborne pathogens.

For body artists, exposure usually happens in the form of **needle sticks, pigment splatter, or blood splatter** while working.

This means that you have a risk of contracting a bloodborne pathogens disease because you handle needles (**sharps**) and work in close contact with blood, saliva, and other bodily fluids.

The risk of contracting a bloodborne pathogens disease from a needle stick or pigment splatter during body art is low.

Sharps

"Sharps" are objects that can penetrate the skin or mucous membrane such as needles and razor blades. Sharps can cause a needle stick, for example:

- Accidental puncture
- Tampering with needles
- Dropping a needle
- Broken/sheared contaminated sharps. Contaminated sharps must never be sheared or broken
- Recapping, bending, or removing needles from fixed assemblies. Avoid these actions to prevent a needle stick

Blood and OPIM

Blood and saliva are the two potentially infectious materials you are most likely to come in contact with in body art (tattoos, lip tattoos, piercings). It is important to wear goggles or an eye shield to protect your eyes, and a face mask to protect your nose and mouth from any **pigment or blood splatter**. Small amounts of pigment may splatter you and/or your client while you work. This splatter may contain blood or saliva (if performing a lip procedure). If pigment splatter does come in contact with your eyes, nose, or mouth, flush them immediately and thoroughly with water for 15 minutes.

OPIM stands for Other Potentially Infectious Materials. This is a list of bodily materials that can harbor and transmit disease between you and another person. **You are extremely unlikely to come in contact with most of these other fluids in the body art workplace,** however it is important to know what they are.

OPIM: Other Potentially Infectious Materials

OPIM List

- **Semen**
- **Vaginal secretions**
- **Cerebrospinal fluid** (the clear fluid that surrounds your brain and spine)
- **Synovial fluid** (a gooey liquid between your joints)
- **Pleural fluid** (lung fluid)
- **Pericardial fluid** (the cushioning liquid that surrounds your heart)
- **Urine**
- **Peritoneal fluid** (a lubricating fluid found in your stomach)
- **Vomit**
- **Amniotic fluid** (fluid that surrounds and nourishes babies in pregnant women)
- **Saliva**
- **Any body fluid visibly contaminated with blood**
- **All body fluids in situations where it is difficult or impossible to differentiate between body fluids**
- **Unfixed/detached organs**

What is Cross Contamination?

Preventing cross contamination is one of the most important practices you can learn to break the Chain of Infection and avoid exposure. If you never allow germs to cross over in your area, you will greatly decrease the chances of spreading disease. We will learn more about preventing cross contamination later.

Example: Touching clean objects with dirty gloves

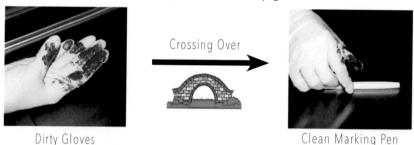

Dirty Gloves

Clean Marking Pen

Cross contamination is the act of infectious agents *crossing over* from something dirty to something clean.

Here are some other common ways technicians cross contaminate and increase the risk of infection:

Touching the following with dirty gloves:
- Getting more supplies while wearing dirty gloves
- Answering the door
- Getting a mirror for the client
- Answering a cell phone, office phone, or checking a text message
- Touching a garbage lid
- Taking before & after photos
- Opening drawers to get products
- Scratching your head/touching your face

Vocabulary		
Chain of Infection	Portal of Exit	Pigment Splatter
Infectious Agent	Means of Transmission	
Reservoir	OPIM	

Diseases to Avoid Contact with Others

It is common courtesy not to get other people sick if you have an infection, however you should really, **really** stay home if you have the following infections:

- Cold, influenza or other respiratory illness accompanied by a fever
- Strep throat
- Pink eye
- Whooping cough
- Chicken pox
- Mumps
- Tuberculosis
- Impetigo or bacterial skin infection
- Head lice
- Scabies or crabs

These infections are listed by the California State Board of Cosmetology as diseases to avoid coming in to work with! Some states will even **require** that you stay home; and if you are an employer, they may require that your employees stay home if you learn that they have these infections.

Chapter 2 Vocabulary:

Chain of Infection
Infectious Agent
OPIM
Acute Stage
Declining Stage
Convalescent Stage

Portal of Exit
Means of Transmission
Portal of Entry
Susceptible Host
Endogenous Infection
Exogenous Infection

Pigment Splatter
Reservoir
Nosocomial Infection
Opportunistic Infection
Incubation Stage
Prodromal Stage

Chapter 2: Test Your Knowledge Questions

1. A pathogen's "path" to disease is called:

   a. Chain of Infection
   b. Path of Infection
   c. Link to Disease
   d. Stairway to Disease

2. What are the components of the Chain of Infection?

3. True or False: For a pathogen, a reservoir is home.

4. Which of the following is not a Portal of Exit for a pathogen?

   a. A wound
   b. Saliva
   c. A sneeze
   d. Hair

5. True or False: Disease can be transmitted through contact with contaminated objects.

6. What does OPIM stand for?

7. How do you protect your face from OPIM during permanent cosmetic procedures?

8. Which of the following is the most likely OPIM that you may encounter in the body art workplace?

  a. Urine
  b. Saliva
  c. Vomit
  d. Peritoneal Fluid

9. True or False: The only Portal of Entry for pathogens is through broken skin.

10. What is a susceptible host? Give 2 examples.

11. The Chain of Infection can be cut...

  a. At any step
  b. At the Portal of Exit
  c. At the Portal of Entry
  d. Cannot be cut

12. True or False: An endogenous infection can be spread from one person to another.

13. Which of the following is not an exogenous infection?

  a. The flu
  b. Radiation poisoning
  c. The common cold
  d. Cancer

14. True or False: Nosocomial/Hospital Acquired infections can only be exogenous.

15. Opportunistic infections usually occur...

  a. When the body's immune system is weak
  b. At any time in anyone
  c. Only in people with AIDS
  d. None of the above

16. Which of the following statements about the incubation stage is false?

  a. This is the stage where the person begins to show symptoms
  b. This stage can range from a few minutes to many years
  c. This stage occurs after the Chain of Infection has been completed
  d. All of the above are true

17. True or False: During the prodromal stage, symptoms become apparent and are specific to the pathogen causing the disease.

18. What is the acute stage of infection?

19. True or False: For body artists, s needle stick or pigment splatter is the most likely form of exposure to Bloodborne pathogens

20. Which stage of infection is the "healing" stage (when the body finishes fighting disease causing pathogens)?

    a. Declining Stage
    b. Acute Stage
    c. Convalescent Stage
    d. Incubation Stage

Chapter 2: Bonus Exercise

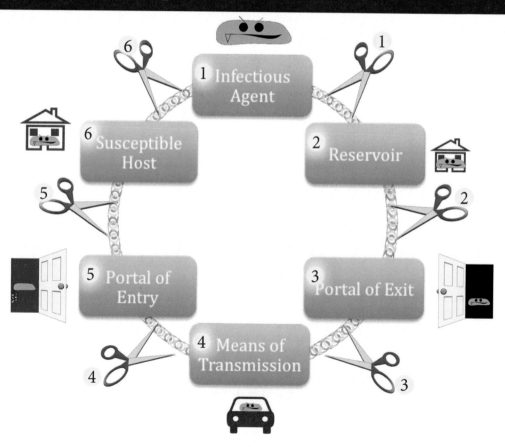

Chapter 2: Bonus Exercise

List Different Ways (as many as you can!) to Cut The Chain Of Infection at Each Pair of Scissors

1 _____
_____
_____
_____

2 _____
_____
_____
_____

3 _____
_____
_____
_____

4 _____
_____
_____
_____

5 _____
_____
_____
_____

6 _____
_____
_____
_____

Notes

Notes

Chapter 3: Common Infections and Bloodborne Pathogen Diseases

Learning Objectives for This Chapter:

- Know which diseases you are most likely to encounter in the body art workplace
- Learn how each disease is spread
- Learn common symptoms of each disease
- Understand your risk of becoming infected by each disease in the workplace
- Know how infections can affect the quality of your work
- Learn how to prevent client cross contamination

It is important as a professional to know what you are up against. Among the many diseases we encounter every day, these seven infections are of particular importance:

Human Immunodeficiency Virus (HIV)
Hepatitis B
Hepatitis C
Tuberculosis
Herpes simplex type 1
Staph infections and Methicillin-resistant Staphylococcus aureus (MRSA)
Mycobacterium Chelonae infections (M. Chelonae)

These three are all **skin infections** that can affect body art professionals

Other Bloodborne Pathogens (less common):

- Arboviral infections such as Colorado tick fever

- Babesiosis (a malaria-like disease caused by parasites)

- Brucellosis (a fever caused by bacteria in unsterile animal products)

- Creutzfeldt-Jakob disease (a brain disease caused by a specific protein)

- Human T-lymphotropic virus type I (a rare pre-lymphoma virus)

- Leptospirosis (a fever caused by animal bacteria in dirty water)

- Relapsing fevers

- Viral hemorrhagic fever (fever with internal bleeding)

3.1 HIV and AIDS

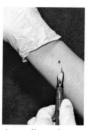

A needle stick is an accidental needle puncture

Human Immunodeficiency Virus (**HIV**) is the virus that leads to Acquired Immunodeficiency Syndrome (**AIDS**). This disease weakens the immune system and lets other harmful diseases (**opportunistic infections**) inside. It may take several years for AIDS to develop in a person who has HIV. AIDS patients are extremely delicate and are at high risk for infection after a body art procedure. It is important to get the client's doctor's permission before performing any work. There is no known vaccine or preventative drug for AIDS—the best way to prevent the spread of this disease is to protect yourself and your clients from **needle sticks**.

<u>Risk</u>: the risk of transmitting HIV in the body art workplace is **very low**

The most likely form of exposure to contaminated blood in body art is a **needle stick**: an accidental puncture from an HIV/AIDS contaminated needle. **The Centers for Disease Control and Prevention (CDC) estimated risk of HIV/AIDS infection with a contaminated needle stick is under 1%**

<u>Transmission</u>: **How is HIV transmitted? How is it NOT transmitted?**

*   HIV **is NOT** transmitted through the air, water, shaking hands or other casual contact
*   HIV **is** spread via blood, semen, and vaginal fluids
*   Sexual contact, needle sharing, and contact with contaminated blood <u>may transmit</u> HIV

<u>Symptoms</u> of HIV Infection	<u>Symptoms</u> of AIDS Infection
Fever	Headaches
Fatigue	Chronic Diarrhea
Swollen lymph nodes	Weight Loss
Coughing and shortness of breath	Skin rashes
	Chills and night sweats

<u>**Control and Prevention**</u> **of HIV/AIDS:**

*   Use standard precautions, work practice controls, engineering controls (more on these later)
*   Avoid needle sticks
*   Avoid blood and sexual contact with HIV/AIDS infected people

48

OSHA Bloodborne Pathogens Standard

What is OSHA?

OSHA stands for the **O**ccupational **S**afety and **H**ealth **A**dministration. This agency handles worker safety in the United States. For healthcare related fields, OSHA has published a standard on bloodborne pathogens titled 29 CFR 1910.1030. This standard outlines procedures for avoiding bloodborne pathogens and related infections. **A copy of the full standard is available on: www.osha.gov**

What is in the standard?

- Rules for making an Exposure Control Plan, which is an emergency plan used in the case of a needle stick
- Information on the transmission, control, and symptoms of bloodborne pathogens diseases
- Engineering and work practice controls, which are strategies (like keeping your sharps container close to your workspace) to prevent injuries
- Handwashing rules
- Sharps container rules
- Personal protective equipment rules (how to use, order to put on and take off, accessibility, laundering, disposal, etc.)
- Sharps handling rules
- Housekeeping, such as decontaminating, disinfecting, and sterilizing objects
- Rules for labeling and disposing of regulated waste
- Rules for record keeping in case of exposure

How do we address the standard?

- This book addresses OSHA's bloodborne pathogens standard from the perspective of body art professionals
- The practices and techniques shown in this book are designed to help you comply with every rule that applies to you.
- When you practice body art at your place of business, use the information in this book to make your workplace safer. Label your containers, keep food away from the treatment area, and use your personal protective equipment correctly to comply!

What is the CDC?

The CDC is the U.S. government agency that protects public health. They watch for outbreaks, respond to emergencies, and continually develop plans to prevent disease

3.2 Hepatitis

Hepatitis is a virus that affects the liver. There are five different forms of Hepatitis: A, B, C, D, and E. Hepatitis B and C pose the highest risk out of these to body art professionals.

Hepatitis A (HAV)

Hepatitis A is caused by fecal contamination in food and water. Rodents and insects carrying the disease excrete infected matter into food and/or water sources, which then infect human beings who eat or drink from that source. HAV is commonly contracted in dirty restaurants; humans who contract the disease feel weak and flu-like, but usually recover on their own (in about 3 months). HAV can be easily prevented by keeping a sanitary workplace.

Hepatitis A is transmitted through contaminated food and water

Hepatitis B (HBV)

Although HIV is more widely feared, Hepatitis B is much more easily transmitted. **Hepatitis B poses a strong risk to body art professionals.** This disease is underreported, meaning many people may not know they have it, or they do know but they do not report it.

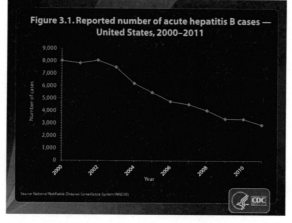

Figure 3.1. Reported number of acute hepatitis B cases — United States, 2000–2011

This figure shows the number of cases of HBV reported to the Centers for Disease Control (CDC) from 1980-2010. The number of unreported cases is esitmated to be very high

50

Hepatitis B Risk, Transmission, Symptoms, and Control/Prevention

Risk: **The CDC estimated risk of HBV infection from a contaminated needle stick is approximately 30% This is a very strong risk for body art professionals.**

Transmission:
- Needle sticks
- Needle sharing/injection drug use
- Contaminated blood transfusions
- Sharing personal items (razors, toothbrushes) contaminated with blood,
- Contact with the open sores of an infected person
- Sexual contact
- *HBV can live in dried blood up to one week*
- Symptoms can surface 1-9 months after exposure

Symptoms:
***There are no symptoms in 30% of infected individuals**

The easiest way to contract HBV is through an accidental puncture with a contaminated needle

- Jaundice
- Fatigue
- Vomiting
- Abdominal pain
- Clay colored stool
- Dark urine
- Joint pain
- Nausea
- Loss of appetite
- HBV may lead to liver scarring, cirrhosis, and even liver cancer

Control and Prevention:
- **A vaccine is available for Hepatitis B. The vaccine is a series of three shots (over 6 months) and is highly recommended for body art professionals**
- The HBV vaccine is known to be safe, but as with any injection you may experience soreness at the injection site.
- **Prevent** HBV by practicing standard precautions, engineering controls, work practice controls
- Avoid sexual contact, sharing personal items, and needle sticks with contaminated individuals

Vaccination is <u>free</u>. Employers are required by Occupational Safety and Health Administration (OSHA) regulations to make the hepatitis B vaccine available at no cost to employees who may be exposed to blood while at work. For more information see Chapter 8, or read the OSHA Bloodborne pathogens standard 1910.1030 (f)(1)(i) and 1910.1030 (f)(1)(ii))

Hepatitis C Risk, Transmission, Symptoms, and Control/Prevention

Hepatitis C is the most common Bloodborne pathogen in the U.S., and is extremely underreported. HCV is known as an **emerging disease**, which means that it could become even more common in the future.

Risk:
- **The CDC estimated risk of HCV infection from a contaminated needle stick is under 2%**

Transmission:
- Sexual contact
- Needle sticks
- Needle sharing—especially with hollow bore needles (the kind used to give injections and draw blood)
- Receiving contaminated blood or organ donations,
- Sharing personal items (razors, toothbrushes) contaminated with blood

Symptoms:
*There are no symptoms in 80% of infected people. If symptoms do emerge, they are similar to HBV:
- Jaundice
- Fatigue
- Vomiting
- Abdominal pain
- Clay colored stool
- Dark urine
- Joint pain
- Nausea
- Loss of appetite
- May lead to liver scarring, chronic liver infections, and cirrhosis

Control and Prevention:
- **No vaccination is available for HCV**
- Avoid needle sticks, sexual contact, needle sharing, and sharing of personal items with contaminated individuals
- Use standard precautions, engineering controls, and work practice controls

Hepatitis D (HDV)

Hepatitis D is actually a **coinfection** with HBV, meaning that you cannot contract Hepatitis D without having Hepatitis B along with it. These diseases can develop together or with HBV developing first.

- HDV is a very serious and often **fatal** disease, especially in Africa, Italy, the Middle East, and South America
- Spread through mucosal (mucous membranes such as your eyes, nose, mouth) contact with infected blood
- Symptoms are flu-like: jaundice, fatigue, vomiting, abdominal pain, clay colored stool, dark urine, joint pain, nausea, loss of appetite
- No vaccine is available for treatment, however the HBV vaccine will prevent HBV carriers from contracting HDV

> You cannot get Hepatitis D without Hepatitis B

You can avoid HDV by avoiding contact with infected blood (via splatter) and by taking the same preventative measures as you would HBV.

Hepatitis E (HEV)

Hepatitis E is also known as enteric hepatitis, meaning that it affects the small intestine. HEV is caused by fecal contamination in food and water. Animals and insects carrying the disease excrete infected matter into food and/or water sources, which then infect human beings who eat or drink from that source. Some of the symptoms of HEV infection include fatigue, vomiting, jaundice, and fever. HEV is more commonly found in underdeveloped countries and is rare in the U.S. There is no vaccination available for HEV, however patients with this disease usually get better on their own with time.

To avoid HEV, avoid eating or drinking from questionable sources, such as dirty water and contaminated food.

Vocabulary	HIV	Hepatitis B (HBV)	Emerging disease
	AIDS	Hepatitis C (HCV)	Coinfection
	Needle Stick	OSHA	
	Centers for Disease Control and Prevention (CDC)		

3.3 Tuberculosis

Tuberculosis is a bacterial infection that affects the lungs. This infection often remains dormant in the body (in the **incubation** stage of infection) for months before symptoms begin to show. Some patients never experience symptoms at all; this kind of infection is called *Latent TB Infection, or LTBI*. LTBI patients are generally not a concern, however those with an active infection of TB, or *TB disease*, can transmit the disease through the air when they speak, sing, cough, or sneeze, expelling infected droplets of fluid from their lungs.

Risk: There is no concrete data for risk following exposure to TB in a body art scenario, however in general risk increases as your proximity to an infected person increases. Do not work on a client with an active TB infection.

Symptoms:
- Chronic cough
- Fever
- Loss of appetite
- Weight loss
- Fatigue
- Night sweats

Transmission:
- Through the air when an infected person coughs, speaks, sings, or sneezes
- Through cross contamination with infected saliva

Control and Prevention:
- Treatment is available with antibiotics for infected individuals
- Infected individuals can wear a special mask to help prevent transmission through the air
- Use standard precautions, engineering controls, and work practice controls

Wear your protective clothing to prevent the spread of germs

Also note that the disinfectant you use to clean surfaces must be tuberculocidal, meaning that the disinfectant kills tuberculosis. We will talk more about disinfectants later.

3.4 Herpes Simplex Type 1 (HSV-1)

Herpes simplex type 1 is the virus that produces cold sores. If you have never seen a cold sore, it is a small/medium lesion on the mouth, lips, or lower facial area filled with fluid. Cold sores often resemble severe acne spots, and can be spread from person to person from contact with the sores or fluid inside. HSV-1 is relevant to body art for those performing lip tattoos or piercings. If a client is prone to cold sores, that means they have this virus. Lip procedures (tattoos, piercings, etc) may be more prone to infections and may cause cold sore break outs. Advise clients to take a preventative medication before their appointment.

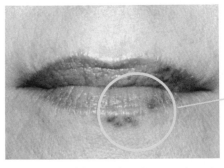

A common cold sore breakout, otherwise known as Herpes Simplex Type 1

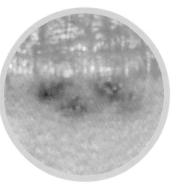

Cold sores up close

Risk: About 1 in 4 people have this virus and are unaware that they have it. HSV-1 is usually contracted during childhood

Symptoms:
- Tingling or itching before sore formation
- Fluid filled, acne like lesions on or around the mouth (cold sores)

Transmission:
- Through cross contamination with infected saliva
- Kissing, sexual contact
- Sharing personal items (drinks, food, lipstick/lip balm, etc)

Some medications can help prevent cold sores, clients should take them prior to lip tattoos or piercings

Control and Prevention:
- Treatment is available with antibiotics for infected individuals, however there is no cure
- Infected individuals can wear a special mask to help prevent transmission through the air
- Use standard precautions, engineering controls, and work practice controls

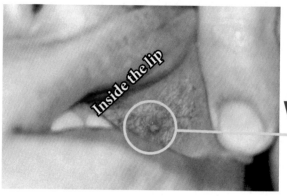

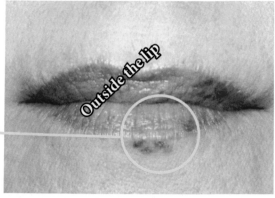

Canker Sore

Cold Sore

Cold sores are caused by the Herpes Simplex Type 1 (HSV1) virus, which causes small lesions (sometimes called fever blisters) on the **outside** of the mouth. Canker sores are NOT caused by HSV1, and occur on the **inside** of the mouth. A canker sore is a small ulcer that forms in the mouth as a result of stress (ex: you accidentally bite the inside of your lip), allergies, or a reaction with one of the many bacteria that live inside the mouth. If a client has a canker sore, avoid working on the inside of the lip until it heals.

3.5 Staph Infections, Double Dipping, and Methicillin-resistant Staphylococcus aureus (MRSA)

Staph infections are skin diseases caused by a type of bacteria called *Staphylococcus aureus* (or "staph" for short) which is very common and caused by cross contamination in body art. Staph infections usually develop within 24 hours of cross contamination with staph bacteria. Remember that this can happen in your office, or at the client's own home.

Risk: There is no concrete data for the risk of staph infections in body art, however considering the ease of transmission, and how common staph infections are in this industry, the risk is not to be taken lightly.

Symptoms:
- Tenderness
- Swelling
- Redness
- Open sores

How to Pronouce It:
Staphylococcus = "staf-ah-low-kah-kus"
Aureus = "aw-ree- us"

Transmission:
- Contact with staph bacteria on an open wound

- Contact with contaminated surfaces

Control and Prevention:
- Treatment is available with antibiotics for infected individuals
- Wash any cuts, fresh tattoos, and/or open skin with soap and water and keep clean and dry
- Always use clean/sterile instruments
- Use standard precautions, engineering controls, and work practice controls
- Always give your client post treatment instructions on how to care for their body art, such as no double dipping with ointment

Double Dipping With Ointment

The most common skin infections are caused by the misuse of post-treatment ointments. Touching a cotton swab to the ointment, applying it, and then using the **same** end of that swab to dip again (**double dipping, see figures 1 and 2**) will spread germs all over the open skin. Never touch a dirty swab to an ointment container, and remind clients to follow the same rules. At home, clients will sometimes use their fingers, this is not allowed!

How to Apply Post-Treatment Ointment

1 Squeeze onto a clean surface

2 Use a clean cotton swab to apply

3 Use a new swab or the clean end to apply more if needed

No double dipping!

Figure 1

Figure 2

Methicillin-resistant Staphylococcus aureus (MRSA) is a special type of staph infection which has developed a resistance to many antibiotics. MRSA is spread easily through contact between open skin and contaminated surfaces. Symptoms include inflammation, pus filled boils, bite-like lesions, and painful red bumps.

MRSA must be treated by a healthcare professional. Special antibiotics are usually given to the patient after boils are drained. Infected clients can have repeat infections as well. To protect yourself and your clients from skin infections, including MRSA, be sure to use only sterile implements, don't double dip, and always work to maintain a clean environment.

Client Cross Contamination

A client just called me and said that she got an infection, did I cause this?

Clients often cross contaminate without realizing it, causing infections after they leave your office. How do you know if you caused the infection, or if they cross contaminated elsewhere?

The answer is that it is hard to know! Usually, most skin infections develop within 24 hours of cross contamination, so if your client showed symptoms of infection within a day of leaving your shop, it may have been you. If not, however, it is more likely that the infection was developed elsewhere.

- Remember that the human body is a reservoir for staph bacteria, the infection could have come from the client scratching their head and then touching the procedure
- Remember that germs are everywhere, the client could have touched an unclean surface and then touched the new tattoo/piercing
- **Remember that the client could have double dipped with their post treatment ointment, contaminating it and causing an infection. This is the most common way clients cross contaminate**

Where can your client pick up an infection after the procedure?	What can you do to prevent this?
Your shop: dirty tools, poor hygiene, dirty surfaces, cross contamination in the office	Use standard precautions, engineering controls, and work practice controls
The client's home: touching dirty objects, surfaces, or pets and then touching the procedure	Advise the client to be careful not to touch the procedure until they wash their hands
The client's body: touching areas which are home to a lot of bacteria, such as body hair, and then touching the procedure	Advise the client to be careful not to touch the procedure until they wash their hands
The client's environment: swimming in contaminated water, using contaminated saunas, gym showers, public areas	Have the client avoid these areas until the skin is fully healed
The client's habits: double dipping with post treatment ointment can contaminate the ointment and cause infection	Make sure your clients know not to double dip! Give them a post treatment instruction list to help them care for their procedure

3.6 Mycobacterium Chelonae infections (M. Chelonae)

M. Chelonae infections made headlines in 2012 when tattoo artists used contaminated ink on clients. In most cases, water was used to dilute black pigment into shades of gray. M. Chelonae bacteria from the water (most likely tap water) contaminated the tattoo ink, which was then put directly into the skin during the procedure. These clients developed severe skin infections that took months to heal. Symptoms include a non-healing, non-spreading wound.

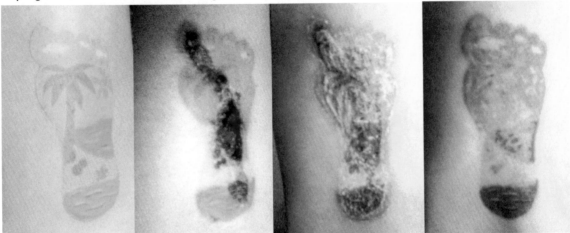

| An ankle tattoo before infection, with contaminated ink | Acute (full blown) infection in the tattooed area from contaminated ink | The skin of the entire tattoo is slowly replaced by new tissue | The infection heals, leaving scarred skin and faded color |

To avoid these infections, make sure you are using the cleanest water possible to dilute your pigments, if you do dilute them. The cleanest water available is sterile water, be sure to use this if it is required in your state. However if this is not available, the next best option is distilled water, which can be purchased at any local grocery store. Sterile glycerin is also a great option if you can find it!

3.7 What Should I Do if I Have a Client With an Infection?

Our most important rule in bloodborne pathogens safety is to work as if every client has a deadly transmittable disease. Therefore you should treat known infected clients the same as any other client. Use the same standard precautions; wear your protective clothing, keep a clean environment, and prevent cross contamination in the workplace.

That being said, **if you have a client that has a rash, inflamed, or infected skin, do not perform the procedure until this area has healed.** You could transfer bacteria from infected skin to non-infected skin, spreading and worsening the condition.

Chapter 3 Summary

Chapter 3 Vocabulary:

HIV
Hepatitis
AIDS
Staph Infection
Needle Stick
Double Dipping

Hepatitis B (HBV)
Tuberculosis
Hepatitis C (HCV)
Staphylococcus Aureus
OSHA
Mycobacterium Chelonae

Emerging disease
Herpes Simplex Type 1 (HSV-1)
Coinfection
MRSA
Centers for Disease Control (CDC)

Chapter 3: Test Your Knowledge Questions

1. All of the following are common infections and Bloodborne pathogens diseases you may encounter in the workplace EXCEPT:

    a. Tuberculosis
    b. HIV/AIDS
    c. Herpes Simplex Type 1
    d. All of the above are infections you may encounter in the workplace

2. True or False: If you get a needle stick from a client who has HIV/AIDS, you are **highly** likely to contract the disease.

3. Which of the following forms of Hepatitis pose the most risk to body art professionals?

    a. Hepatitis B and C
    b. Hepatitis A and D
    c. Hepatitis A and B
    d. Hepatitis C and D

4. True or False: Hepatitis B can be prevented by getting a vaccine.

5. Hepatitis D can only be contracted if you already are infected with...

    a. Hepatitis A
    b. Hepatitis B
    c. Hepatitis C
    d. Hepatitis E

6. What is Tuberculosis(TB) and how is it transmitted?

7. True or False: Any disinfectant can kill TB.

8. True or False: Herpes Simplex Type 1 and cold sores are unrelated.

9. True or False: Cold sores can cause loss of color in the lips.

10. If you have a client with HIV, AIDS, or Hepatitis B, you should:

    a. Refuse to work on them
    b. Tell them a doctor must work on them
    c. Treat them like any other client and follow the precautions in this book
    d. None of the above

11. List some of the ways a client can get an infection at home.

12. True or False: Diluting your ink with dirty water can cause an infection.

13. What does OSHA stand for?

14. How is HIV transmitted?

    a. Through hugs
    b. Through a cough or sneeze
    c. Through sexual contact or exchange of bodily fluids
    d. None of the above

15. HBV is an infection of what part of the human body?

16. HBV can survive in dried blood for up to:

    a. 1 day
    b. 4 days
    c. 7 days
    d. 10 days

61

Notes

Notes

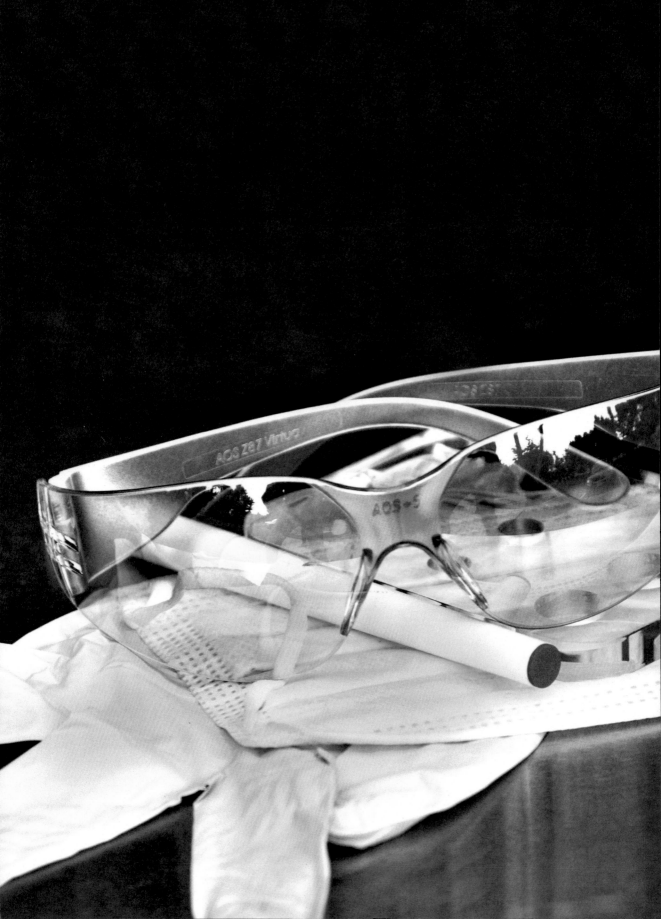

Chapter 4: Engineering Controls and Setting Up a Body Art Workspace

4.1 What are Engineering Controls?

Engineering Controls are objects, designs, or devices that minimize your risk in the workplace. You can "engineer" your body art area to be safer by using items or designs such as:

- Arrangements of the room or workspace
- Sharps containers
- Regulated waste containers or bags
- Signs and labels

4.2 Arranging Your Workspace

First of all, your work area for body art should be separate from all other work areas, reception areas, kitchen areas, and recreation areas. Pathogens native to these areas (such as germs in a kitchen sink, or germs from a recreational couch)must not be allowed to cross over into the work area. Here are some other basic rules for your work area:

- Keep it uncluttered, and free from unrelated equipment and activities
- Should be easy to move around in to prevent tripping/accidents
- Should have non-porous surfaces (smooth and non-absorbent tables, chairs, counters)
- Have adequate lighting
- Have covered trash cans (that open with a foot pedal or motion sensor)
- Install wall dispensers for supplies
- Have a sink close to the work area, for hand washing only. A separate sink should be available (not in the work area) for cleaning/decontaminating items
- Stock as many disposable supplies as possible (using disposables is safer than cleaning and reusing)

Carpet can harbor germs, smooth floors are easier to clean

Floors and Surfaces:
There are two kinds of surfaces in body art:

1. **Clinical contact surfaces:** These are surfaces you can easily cross contaminate (while wearing dirty gloves), such as treatment beds, treatment tables, lamps, chairs, trash cans, etc.

2. **Housekeeping surfaces:** These are your floors, walls, windows, etc.

- Floors, walls, counters, magnifying lamps, tables, chairs, and other surfaces should be smooth and non-absorbent. Carpets and cloth can harbor harmful bacteria and should be avoided. Smooth surfaces are also easier to clean
- You should have good lighting in order to see your work and reduce the risk of injury

Proper lighting is important to prevent accidents and help you clean up

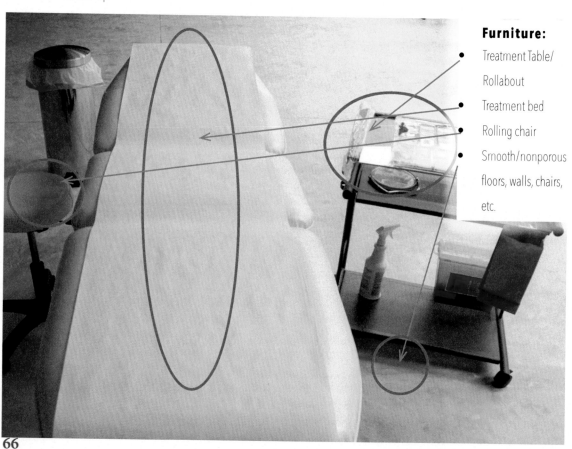

Furniture:
- Treatment Table/ Rollabout
- Treatment bed
- Rolling chair
- Smooth/nonporous floors, walls, chairs, etc.

Glove dispensers make glove access clean and easy

Use Dispensers:

- You can get wall dispensers for most of your equipment, this helps prevent cross contamination as you won't need to rummage through drawers to reach items
- Use a covered trash can opened with a foot pedal or motion sensor
- **Label your containers to make sure you do not confuse chemicals and supplies**

Use Disposable Supplies:

- Disposable supplies and barriers decrease the risk of cross contamination and infection
- Keep your supplies off of your treatment table, only the items you are using should be on the table

Sinks:

- Should be conveniently close to the work area, but at least a few feet away from where you store sterile items, so that items in stored paper packaging will not have a chance of becoming wet and then contaminated
- **Should be for handwashing only, you should have a separate sink for cleaning items**
- If there is only one sink available for both cleaning items and handwashing, keep items that need cleaning in a separate, closed container near the sink until you are going to clean them

Keep dirty implements in a closed, labeled container until you are ready to clean them

Motion-sensing/touchless faucets, paper towel dispensers, and soap dispensers are excellent for avoiding cross contamination during handwashing

Sinks: (continued)

- Keep the sink clear to prevent cross contamination (for example: do not leave cleaning supplies in the sink)
- The sink should have potable hot and cold running water
- Use soap in a single use dispenser (the dispenser container should be disposable)
- If you refill the soap dispenser, first clean it, disinfect it, and allow it to air dry
- Use single use paper hand towels in a dispenser

What About Portable Sinks?

Portable sinks are generally allowed for temporary events. Sometimes they are the only option available. Older buildings may not have plumbing in the immediate area where you work, and if you work special events the only sink may be far away or in a public restroom. If this is the case a portable sink is certainly better than public sinks or no sinks!

Check with your local authorities on their requirements for portable sinks. If they are allowed in your area, make sure that:

- You are using clean potable water to refill the sink

- The waste container is emptied and cleaned at the end of every day

- The waste reservoir is larger than the clean reservoir so that waste water cannot flow back into the clean water

- The sink has hot and cold running water

- The sink water comes out at the same flow rate (water pressure) as plumbed sink water would (this info can be obtained from the sink manufacturer)

4.3 Using Barrier Film for Surfaces

Doctors use barrier film to protect surfaces from cross contamination during a procedure. You can buy barrier film to use as a barrier. **Plastic food wrap is not acceptable because it was not designed to protect against blood and OPIM; therefore it may not provide an adequate barrier.** Cover your drawer handles, magnifying lamp, containers, treatment tables, door handles, and mirror handles before you begin to keep these surfaces clean during a procedure.

Barrier Film

A drawer handle

A mirror

A treatment bed

You can use barrier film on all of these things!

Apply barrier film with clean hands

A treatment table/rollabout

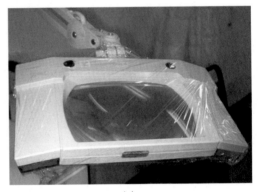

A lamp

Once the procedure is finished and all other items have been cleaned and disposed of, you may remove the film with gloves on.

Removing barrier film with gloves on

Barrier Film on a Coil Machine

- Apply barrier film with clean hands
- Cover everything except the tube and needle
- Cover clip cords
- Cover power box

Any part above the tube vice that is not disposable must be cleaned, disinfected, and sterilized according to manufacturer's instructions

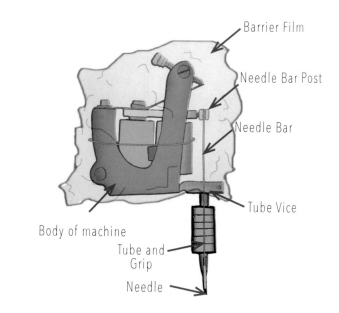

Barrier Film

Needle Bar Post

Needle Bar

Tube Vice

Body of machine

Tube and Grip

Needle

Barrier Film on a Rotary Machine

- Apply barrier film with clean hands
- Cover everything except the tube and needle
- Cover cords
- Cover power box
- Cover the motor
- You can buy multiple casings to use while others are being sterilized

Any parts that are not disposable must be cleaned, disinfected, and sterilized (if possible) according to manufacturer's instructions

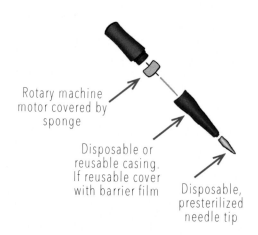

Rotary machine motor covered by sponge

Disposable or reusable casing. If reusable cover with barrier film

Disposable, presterilized needle tip

4.4 Single Use Items and Completely Sterilizable Items

Many piercing professionals work with single use needles and other instruments. These tools typically do not need to be wrapped in barrier film. In addition, very traditional forms of tattooing and permanent makeup use hand tools; these are all single use instruments or have an autoclavable handle attached. Barrier film is usually not required for these tools as they are either 100% disposable or can be dimantled completely and sterilized.

100% Single Use

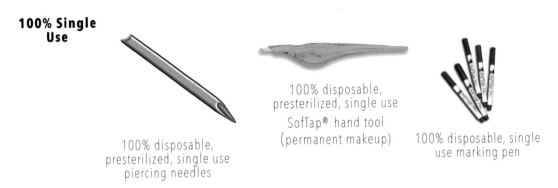

100% disposable, presterilized, single use piercing needles

100% disposable, presterilized, single use SofTap® hand tool (permanent makeup)

100% disposable, single use marking pen

100% Sterilizable

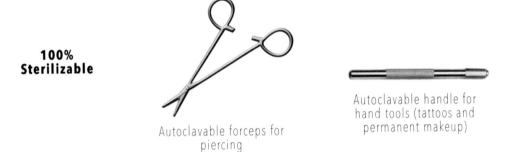

Autoclavable forceps for piercing

Autoclavable handle for hand tools (tattoos and permanent makeup)

Other notes:
- Approved ASTM standard body jewelry (piercing jewelry) that is not damaged, pitted or corroded can usually be sterilized and reused, however please check the regulations for your area
- Always dispose of single use razors (for shaving prior to tattooing) in the sharps container

4.5 Pillows, Drapes, and Treatment Trays

Pillows

If you use pillows for your clients during a procedure, you must cover them with paper beforehand, and always change this paper between clients. Pillows should be changed and the cases washed every day.

Client Drapes

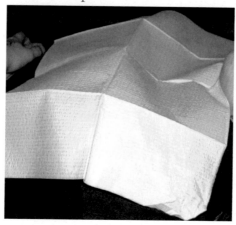

Use disposable client drapes to protect client's clothing from any splatter. Dispose of these drapes after each use, and use a new drape for every client.

Disposable Treatment Trays

Plastic or paper single use, disposable treatment trays are available as an alternative to stainless steel instrument trays. Reusable trays are acceptable as long as they can be easily disinfected. Any reusable tray is considered a clinical contact surface and must be able to be cleaned with an intermediate level disinfectant.

4.6 Sharps

Your **sharps container** is a puncture-proof container where you dispose of your used needles. It is important to use a sharps container to prevent injuries to anyone who handles garbage, intentionally or unintentionally. The container you use must follow a few basic rules to keep people safe. It must be leak-proof, puncture proof (so your needles don't poke through), brightly colored, and labeled to let others know that sharp objects are inside. You can buy sharps containers from various body art suppliers or a medical supply shop.

- **Your Sharps Container:**

- Must be located close to the immediate area where the sharps are used

- Must be maintained in an upright position

- **There is a safety line near the top of the container that you can fill it up to. Never allow the container to fill up past this line**

- Must be able to be closed securely when full

- Must be entirely leak proof

- Must be puncture resistant

BIOHAZARD

Using a wall mount for your sharps container is a good way to keep it from getting knocked over. Containers are easily removed/changed too!

- Must be labeled "Biohazard" with the international biohazard symbol or color-coded in a noticeable way, such as with an orange or orange-red label with lettering and symbols in a contrasting color

- **Contaminated sharps must not be bent, recapped, removed, sheared, or broken**

- **Sharps are considered regulated waste**

- Sharps are the most dangerous item you handle at work

Why?

These rules are in place to prevent the liklihood of your sharps container spilling over, breaking, or overflowing. If contaminated needles spill out onto the floor, they could cause injury to you, your clients, or others that work in the area.

The reason your sharps container must be close to your treatment area is so that you can avoid transporting contaminated needles long distances. You have more of a chance of accidentally sticking another person or yourself if you are walking down a long hallway with a dirty needle in your hand than if you are just turning to the right or left to reach your sharps container

Your sharps container must be a bright color to let others know that there are sharps in the area, and also to prevent it from being knocked over.

What Do I Do When My Sharps Container is Full?

The point of a sharps container is to keep sharp, contaminated objects away from you, your clients, and people who handle medical waste. When your sharps container is full, close it securely and drop off or send it off in the mail to a medical waste recycling company. Some health departments and fire stations will also recycle medical waste for free or a small fee. Keep your receipts as records of proper sharps disposal.

4.7 Regulated Waste

Regulated waste is any kind of waste that is contaminated with enough OPIM to cause a hazard to the workplace. Contaminated laundry or disposables are considered regulated waste when you can squeeze a drop of blood from them.

- **If you can squeeze one drop of blood or Other Potentially Infectious Material (OPIM) from gauze, tissue, a labcoat, face mask, or gloves, you cannot throw these items in the garbage, you must follow the procedure below**
- **If an item has enough dried blood or OPIM caked on it to cause the release of powder/particles in the air, the item is regulated waste**
- **Contaminated needles are considered regulated waste. Used needles are disposed of in sharps containers and follow sharps container rules**

How to dispose of regulated waste:

1. Place in a red bag or brightly colored container

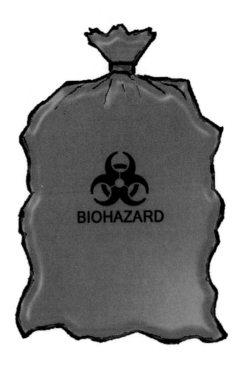

- The bag or container must be closeable and leak proof
- The container must be red or have a fluorescent orange or orange/red label with letters on the label in a contrasting color. This and the biohazard symbol will indicate regulated waste

2. Ship this waste to a medical waste disposal center as soon as possible, and no later than seven days. After seven days infectious material may begin to spread from the container to other areas, increasing the possibility of infection.

 ## 4.8 Signs and Labels

Signs and labels are a very effective method for protecting everyone in your body art facility. Label the following items and be sure to keep dates and notices current:

- Antiseptics
- Disinfectants
- Sharps containers
- Chemicals
- Supply containers (drawers for gloves, sterile needles, ink, forceps, etc)
- Miscellaneous supplies
- Post signs in your office for no smoking, no food or drink, and no animals (except service animals, as required by law)

Chapter 4 Summary

Chapter 4 Vocabulary:

Engineering Controls   Regulated waste   Sharps Container
Clinical Contact Surface   Housekeeping Surface

Chapter 4: Test Your Knowledge Questions

1. All of the following are sharps container rules you should follow EXCEPT:

    a. Must be leak-proof
    b. Must be puncture resistant
    c. Must be at least 5-quart
    d. Must be labeled with the international biohazard symbol

2. True or False: Contaminated needles are considered regulated waste

3. Which of the following items should you label to prevent accidents in the workplace?

    a. Disinfectants
    b. Antiseptics
    c. Bleach
    d. Miscellaneous supplies
    e. All of the above

4. True or False: You can throw regulated waste in the regular garbage as long as it is in a sealed, brightly colored and labeled container

5. A portable sink is acceptable to use if...

    a. A clean plumbed sink is unavailable
    b. Clean, potable water is being used in the reservoir and being changed every day
    c. It has hot and cold running water
    d. It is allowed by your local authories
    e. Any one of the above
    f. All of the above

6. What is the difference between a clinical contact surface and a housekeeping surface? Give two examples of each

7. True or False: You should have at least two sinks at your facility: one for handwashing, and one for decontaminating items

8. True or False: You don't need to cover pillows if pillowcases are washed at the end of each day

Notes

Notes

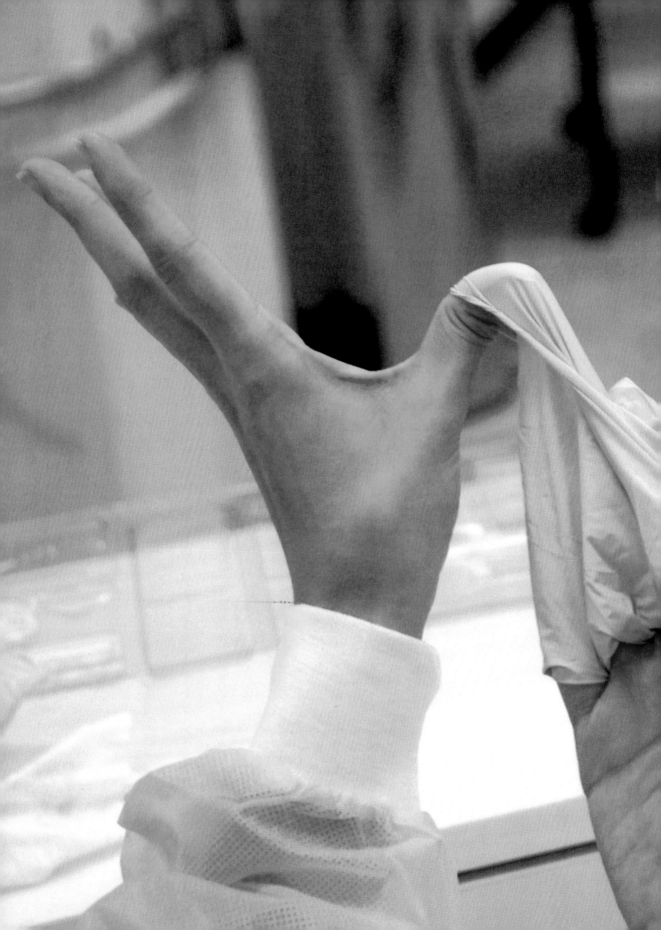

Chapter 5: Work Practice Controls

5.1 What are Work Practice Controls?

Work Practice Controls are everyday actions and methods you perform to minimize injury and the risk of exposure to bloodborne pathogens.

Examples:

- **Using standard precautions**
- Throwing away used needles in your sharps container before cleaning the rest of your work area
- **Contaminated needles and other sharps must not be bent, recapped, or broken**
- Not eating, drinking, or smoking in the work area
- Washing your hands
- Wearing **Personal Protective Equipment (PPE)**

Learning Objectives for This Chapter:

- Define work practice controls
- Develop reliable work practice controls
- Define and follow standard precautions
- Define and know the use, types, and order of donning and discarding PPE
- Define cross contamination
- Understand the importance and methods of preventing cross contamination

5.2 Standard and Universal Precautions

Standard Precautions refers to the methods developed by the Centers for Disease Control and Prevention (CDC) to minimize exposure to infection in the workplace. **The main philosophy behind these precautions is to treat all blood and bodily fluids (even if they do not contain blood) as if they are contaminated and dangerous.** Part of standard precautions involves:

- Wearing Personal Protective Equipment (PPE)
- Proper sharps (needle) handling and disposal
- Proper hand washing
- Proper handling of regulated waste
- Proper decontamination, disinfection and sterilization
- Preventing cross contamination

Another set of precautions/methods, called Universal Precautions, deals with treating only **blood** (and fluids visibly contaminated with blood) as infected. **In contrast, standard precautions treat <u>every</u> fluid as infectious.** In this chapter we will begin with methods to best prepare for your body art procedure. This includes gathering supplies, handwashing, Personal Protective Equipment (PPE), preparing the client, and preventing cross contamination.

5.3 Gathering Your Supplies

It is very important that your client sees that your office is clean and ready to work in. When gathering your supplies, get any tools, ink, or needles you might need for the procedure, take what you need, and put the containers away. You should not have any product containers in your treatment area.

Set up all of these items in the presence of your client, so that they can see that you are using new, clean materials.

When handling needles and other single use items, check the package first to make sure it is clean and intact before opening. If the package is torn, punctured, or soiled, throw it away and use a different one.

Dispense what you need and put away containers!

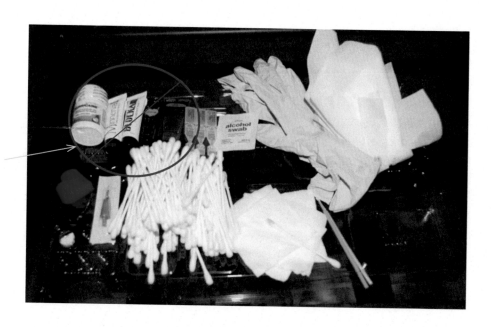

5.4 Handwashing

Handwashing is the single most important action you can do to prevent the spread of infection. Antimicrobial soap, running water, and friction will mechanically and chemically remove germs from your hands. **Handwashing should take no less time than 30 seconds.**

When should you wash your hands?

- Before beginning to work on a client
- If you leave your treatment zone, for any reason
- Whenever you need to change your gloves, see Page 94

Can I just wear gloves instead?

Gloves are not a substitute for hand hygiene. You need to wash your hands before and after using gloves to protect your clients from germs on your hands!

Repeated washing makes my hands dry, what can I do?

Use hand lotion to keep your hands from becoming too dry, but make sure it is not petroleum based, that kind of lotion can damage your gloves!

What About Hand Sanitizer?

Hand sanitizer is actually an antiseptic, it is meant for cleansing the skin. Hand sanitizers usually contain 60-80% alcohol, which kills most germs found on your hands. This is very effective for hands that are not visibly soiled. Most hand sanitizers do contain moisturizer, which is an added benefit. You can use hand sanitizer as a supplement to handwashing, but not a replacement. Hand sanitizer will not work on visibly soiled hands. Soap and water is still the best option available for hand hygiene.

1. Approach your sink, making sure none of your uniform (PPE) touches the sink

2. Remove any jewelry (jewelry traps and holds bacteria that can contaminate your hands. It also increases the risk of tearing your gloves)

3. Gather antimicrobial soap on your hands. <u>See the section on soaps in the next few pages to learn how to choose a soap.</u> You need about 1 teaspoon of soap for each time you wash your hands. Use hands free soap dispensers if possible

Use paper towels to turn knobs on sinks

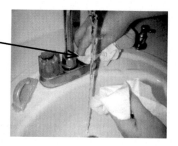

No cloth towels!

4. Use warm water; this helps remove germs and decontaminates your hands more quickly than cool water. Hands-free faucets are the best to use for body art and are readily available Alternatively, if you have a traditional sink with knobs, use a clean, dry paper towel to turn on the faucet. Do not use cloth towels, they can grow harmful bacteria that can be transferred to your hands when you touch them

Getting Soap

5.	Point your fingers downwards, and use your opposite hand to scrub the back of your hand. Repeat with the other side

6.	Interlace your fingers to scrub in between, then interlock your fingers and rub them against your palms

7.	Carefully and gently clean under your nails with a hand brush (you only need to do this at the beginning and end of the day)

8.	Rinse your hands, lather again and wash your palms and wrists with your fingers in a circular motion, don't forget to wash your thumbs!

9.	Wash your wrists and forearms with firm, circular motions up to the elbow

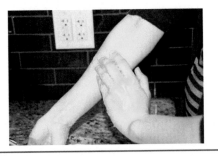

10.	Rinse your hands with cool water to close your pores, this makes your skin more difficult for germs to penetrate

11.	Dry your hands with a paper towel, then your forearms

12.	If using a traditional sink, (a sink without automatic sensors use a **second dry** paper towel to turn off the water, **no wet towels!** (The first paper towel you used to dry your hands would now be wet, so make sure to get a new one)

If you are washing because your procedure was interrupted, do not touch anything until you have new gloves on! You may not touch the garbage to throw away your paper towels, so use a garbage can with a foot pedal or motion sensor

The sink at which you wash your hands should be close to your treatment area; this helps prevent the spread of germs

Know Your Soaps!

 There are many different kinds of soaps. Some are used for hand washing, some for client's skin, and some for cleaning surfaces. Let's talk about the different forms that soap comes in. What is the difference between foaming soap, bar soap, liquid soap, and powdered soap?

Soap Type (Physical Form)	What is it?	Main Use	Effectiveness at Removing Germs	Cost Effectiveness	Carbon Footprint
Bar Soap	Traditional bar of soap used for regular handwashing	Home	Effective with longer wash times (30 seconds), but can harbor germs when left wet	Inexpensive, but may not be allowed in some areas	Low, but may use more water than other methods
Liquid Soap	Also called detergent, the liquid form of soap	Home, office, public restrooms	Good, uses less water than bar soap	Expensive, you tend to use more than you need	Highest
Foaming Soap	Liquid soap in a dispenser which foams the soap	Home, office, public restrooms	Great, it's pre-lathered so you get effective soap right out of the bottle	Expensive, but because it dispenses much less soap, it lasts you longer	Medium
Powdered Soap	Dried soap flakes and crystals, very abrasive and tough on skin	Office and industrial (removing engine grease from hands)	Great, the scrubbing action of the powder removes tough germs	Inexpensive	Lowest

Know Your Soaps!

What's the difference between plain soap, antimicrobial soap, antibacterial soap, and green soap?

Soap Type (Chemical Form)	What is it?	Main Use	Effectiveness at Removing Germs	Cost Effectiveness
Plain Soap	Traditional soap with no additives, only removes germs with friction/rubbing	Home	Effective	Inexpensive, but may not be allowed in some areas
Antibacterial Soap	Removes most bacteria	Home, office, public restrooms	Good, kills most bacteria	Expensive
Antimicrobial Soap	Removes most microbes, including bacteria, viruses, fungi, and protozoa	Home, office, public restrooms	Best, kills most germs	Expensive
"Green" Soap, also called "tattooist's soap"	Vegetable based soap, (instead of animal fats) It isn't usually green, it is named for its vegetable base	Body Art, used for client skin cleansing, pre-soaking implements for sterilization, general cleaning	Good, mild antimicrobial agent, non-irritating	Inexpensive, used as an antiseptic for client skin cleansing and general cleaning

Which is Best?
All soaps have their pros and cons, but all are effective as long as you use them! It comes down to personal preference; cost, effectiveness, regulations, even scent, look, and feel! Choose what's allowed, safest, gentlest, and the most effective.

Soaps With Moisturizers
Dry skin from constant handwashing can become uncomfortable and even painful! Look for soaps with moisturizers, or purchase lotions to keep your hands comfortable throughout the day!

5.5 Personal Protective Equipment (PPE)

After your room is set up and you are ready to work, you need to wash your hands and put on your **Personal Protective Equipment** (PPE). **PPE is safety gear we use to protect ourselves from exposure to Bloodborne pathogens.** For body art professionals this includes closed toed shoes, a labcoat or other protective clothing (preferably long sleeved and high necked), gloves, a face mask, and goggles or eye shields. We will go over all of these, but first let's go over the order in which these need to be done. This is the order you should get into the habit of when setting yourself up:

What Order Do I Do This In?

After washing your hands:

1. Put on your labcoat

2. Put on your face mask

3. Put on your glasses with side shields, goggles, or other protective eyewear

4. Put on your gloves

Begin client prep!

1: Put on Your Labcoat

While there are many styles of PPE (aprons, long sleeved shirts, smocks, gowns, etc), the safest option is a long sleeved labcoat with a high neck, able to be covered by gloves so that no skin is exposed. These styles offer the most protection from splatter. If you cannot stand long sleeves, take extra care to wash your arms up to the elbow between clients, and make sure you do not have any open skin/cuts.

Disposable labcoats and aprons are a great option as long as they protect you from splatter. Any protective clothing that you reuse must be changed after each client, put in a hamper and washed at the end of the day. Some practitioners keep a washer and dryer in their facility to make this easier, this is an excellent idea because if laundry is washed promptly it cannot become a reservoir for infectious agents. Whoever handles dirty laundry should wear gloves and avoid touching soiled labcoats as much as possible. Remember that a labcoat is not a substitute for personal hygiene, and is limited to splatter protection only.

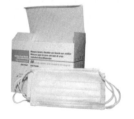

2: Put on Your Face Mask

Face masks can be dome shaped, pleated, elastic, tie-back, or have ear loops. Some face masks come in special combos with eye shields as well. The mask type you choose should fit well, be comfortable, and most importantly, it should protect you from any splatter or airborne pathogens. The FDA recommends that masks have a 95% or higher bacterial filtration efficiency. This means that your mask should filter out 95% of germs that land on it. This information is usually available on the box your masks came in. Remember that masks are limited in that they only filter airborne pathogens. They do not protect against needle sticks or other risks.

1.	Handle the mask at the edges, not the body 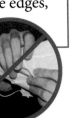	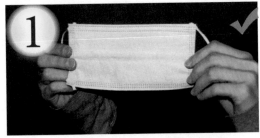
2.	Place the ear loops on your ears, put the elastic band behind your head, or tie the strings behind your head, depending on the mask	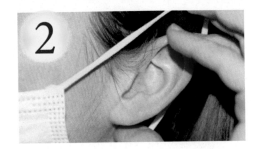
3.	Adjust the mask so the top rests on the bridge of your nose and the bottom covers your chin	
4.	If you wear glasses, your glasses can rest on top of your mask	
5.	Do not pull the mask down onto your neck or up onto your forehead at any time, this can allow any splatter on your mask to come in contact with your skin	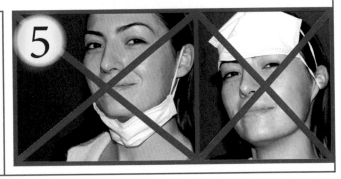

3: Put on Your Protective Eyewear

- Eye protection must provide both front and side protection from splatter

- Your eyeglasses can be used as protection as long as you use side shields with them. Side shields are special plastic shields that attach to the sides of your glasses

- Any eye protection you use during a procedure must be washed thoroughly with soap and hot water after each client

- You may disinfect your eyewear before each new client by using a disinfectant spray (more on disinfectants later)

- Face shields are another alternative to glasses and goggles. These clear shields cover your entire face and protect it from splatter. You should also wear a face mask with these shields, however, as they do not protect your mouth and nose from airborne pathogens. Some face masks come with shields, like the one pictured below.

4: Put on Your Gloves

Nitrile gloves

Gloves are available in a variety of materials, colors, and sizes. Make sure you select gloves that do not irritate your skin (or your clients' skin, if they are allergic to latex) and that fit your hands. The most commonly used gloves for body art are nitrile or latex gloves. If you tend to perspire a lot under your gloves, try powdered gloves or powder your hands with talc before gloving.

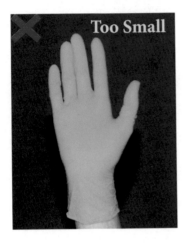

Too Small

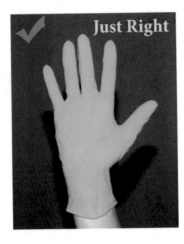

Just Right

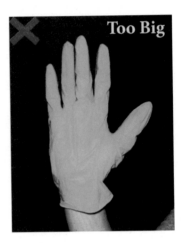

Too Big

Keep your gloves within easy access and in a cool, dark place. Prolonged exposure to the sun, heat, or florescent light can make your gloves more susceptible to ripping, tearing, and decomposition. Remember that gloves do not protect against needle sticks.

Rings, bracelets, watches, and other hand and wrist jewelry must be removed before you wash your hands and put on gloves. Jewelry holds pathogenic bacteria that can be transferred to an open wound and increases your risk of puncturing gloves.

To put on your gloves:
1. Open the glove at the cuff
2. Put your hand inside
3. Pull the glove completely on, being careful not to tear the glove
4. Repeat for the other side

93

When Do You Change Your Gloves?

- Between clients, (after cleaning up and washing your hands)

- When gloves become dirty, sticky, or tacky. If they become sticky or tacky this is a sign that the glove surface is beginning to deteriorate

- **When you leave your treatment area for any reason**

- If they become contaminated with potentially infectious matter (OPIM: blood, saliva, etc) during a treatment

- If they become torn or punctured

Change your gloves if they become dirty or tacky

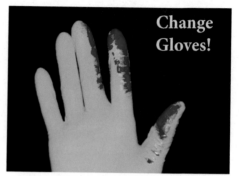

Change your gloves if they get blood or OPIM on them

NEVER wash gloves

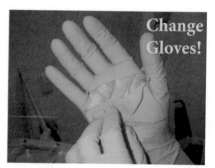

Change your gloves if they become torn

1. Use the fingers of your gloved right hand to pinch the _outside_ cuff of your left glove

2. Pull off your left glove

Think "Glove on glove, skin on skin."

3. Use the clean, ungloved fingers of your left hand to reach _inside_ the cuff of your right glove

4. Pull off your right glove

5. Wash your hands and dry them thoroughly

6. Put on a new pair of gloves

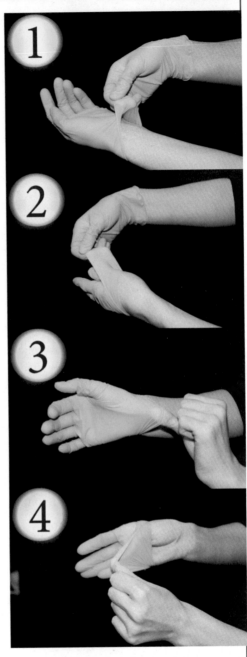

5.6 Body Art Client Prep

1: Drape

Ink Splatter on a Drape

- Use a disposable paper drape to keep any splatter off of your client's clothing
- Drapes also protect any other open skin (acne or cuts for example) from contact with splatter, blood, saliva, or other potentially infectious material

2: Cleanse

- Always cleanse the client's skin before beginning with antimicrobial soap and water, or an **antiseptic**, which is a chemical soap made specifically for skin cleansing. It stops the growth and reproduction of germs
- Cleansing removes any germs on the skin, which is important because needles can push these germs inside, increasing the risk of infection
- Use cotton swabs for hard to reach areas
- Take extra care if cleansing near the eyes. Do not get any antiseptic into the eyes
- A popular skin cleanser for body art is green soap, which is a liquid soap mixture of alcohol and vegetable glycerin

3: Begin

- Begin designing and blueprinting your procedure as needed. Remember that items used on the client's skin cannot be reused. That means that any makeup pencils (permanent makeup), surgical pens for marking, and any stencils used must be **single use only**. These items can transfer bacteria from client to client
- Remember that if you leave your treatment zone for any reason you need to wash and prepare all over again, so make sure you have enough supplies on your treatment table to avoid leaving
- You should not have any product containers in your treatment area, you can contaminate clean products easily while working

Antiseptics and Skin Prep

Choice, Use, and Storage of Antiseptics

An antiseptic is a type of cleanser/antimicrobial soap that slows or stops the growth of microorganisms on the skin. It is used to prepare the skin for a procedure. Some common antiseptics are alcohols, iodine, and hydrogen peroxide. It is important to cleanse the skin with antimicrobial soap and water or an antiseptic to prevent germs from entering the body during a procedure.

How to Choose an Antiseptic

Choose an antiseptic that is effective at killing germs and is gentle on the skin. Many foaming antimicrobial soaps and alcohol wipes are easy to find and are great antiseptics.

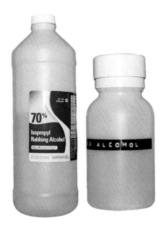 

Green soap, or tattooist's soap, is a mild antiseptic that contains a medium amount of alcohol. You can use this to cleanse the skin before a procedure, but do not use it around the eyes or mucous membranes, as it can cause irritation.

How to Use an Antiseptic

Follow the instructions on your antiseptic package. Throw away the item you used to apply antiseptic to the skin (wipe, gauze, etc). For alcohol wipes, simply wipe the treatment area and throw away the wipe. Do not share alcohol wipes, once used they can be vectors for bloodborne pathogens!

If you use green soap, mix with water according to the manufacturer's instructions, apply to damp gauze, and cleanse the skin. Some practitioners put the soap into a spray or foaming soap bottle to make this easier. Take care to not touch the soap/spray bottle to a client's skin, the nozzle can harbor pathogens and then transfer them between clients.

Do NOT touch nozzles to client's skin

Label your antiseptics

How to Store Antiseptics
Store antiseptics in airtight containers, away from light, to keep them clean and effective. Label them with their name and date purchased so that you know how old solutions are and if/when they must be replaced. When you buy refills for bottles, make sure to wash the bottles thoroughly before filling with new solution.

To Shave or Not To Shave? That is the Question!
Many tattoo artists shave the skin before starting the procedure. This makes the skin easier to see and work with, but it also prevents germs that live on (and around) hairs from getting into the fresh tattoo. **Shaving can help prevent infection, but it is not necessary in all cases**. If the area to be worked on is relatively small (most piercings, ankle tattoos, permanent makeup) and/or does not have a significant amount of body hair, the risk of infection is much less than that of larger pieces. In some situations, such as permanent makeup, shaving defeats the purpose of the appointment; clients come in to have their eyebrows tattooed, not shaved off. In many cases, shaved eyebrows do not grow back. Thorough cleansing of the skin should be enough to prevent infection for these instances.

Disposable Razors ONLY!
If you decide to shave the treatment area, cleanse the area with an antiseptic first, and use only brand new, single use, disposable razors. Reusing/sharing razors can trasmit bloodborne pathogens such as Hepatitis, Herpes Simplex Type 1, and various skin infections. Dispose of used razors immediately in a sharps container. Alternatively, you may use a razor with a reusable handle and detachable tips, as long as the handle is sterilized/high level disinfected between uses and the blades are disposed of in the sharps container after each client.

Your Setup Checklist: Remember to...

- Prepare your office: cover clean surfaces you might touch with barrier film, cover pillows and headrests

- Gather any tools, pigment/ink, jewelry, and antiseptic you might need for the procedure, take what you need, and put the containers away. You should not have any product containers in your treatment area
- Greet your client, ensure all paperwork has been filled out, take any before photos if you need them, and seat the client in the work area

Tie back long hair before preparing your office

Then, in this order: (see opposite page as well)
1. Wash your hands

2. Put on your labcoat

3. Put on your face mask

4. Put on your glasses with side shields, goggles, or other protective eyewear

5. Put on your gloves

6. Prep the client and begin

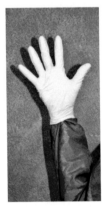

Your gloves should cover the cuffs of your labcoat to prevent any pigment splatter on your wrists or forearms

Setup Order: What Order to Dress, Wash, and Prep

Wash your
hands

Put on your lab coat

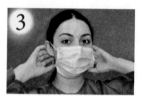

Put on your face mask

Put on your goggles

Put on your gloves

Prep the client

5.7 What is Cross Contamination?

What is Cross Contamination?

Cross contamination means that an object has become tainted with bacteria from an unclean surface. In other words, germs have **crossed over** from a dirty implement to a clean one, **contaminating** the object. This happens when you touch a clean object, such as a doorknob or cell phone, with dirty gloves. There are many ways a technician can accidently contaminate a clean implement.

Common Ways Body Artists Cross Contaminate:

- **Getting more ink/pigment while wearing dirty gloves**

- **Getting more water to dampen gauze and cotton swabs**

- **Getting ointment for the client**

- **Answering the door**

- **Answering a cell phone, office phone, or checking a text message**

- **Touching a garbage lid**

- **Taking before & after photos**

- **Opening drawers to get products**

- **Scratching your head/touching your face**

If you do any of these while wearing dirty gloves, or while not wearing gloves, you could allow pathogens to contaminate surfaces and infect you or or client.

5.8 Preventing Cross Contamination

- No food, drinks, smoking, or pets in the treatment area except as required by the Americans with Disabilities Act

- Protect any open wounds you may have with bandages and PPE before working on a client

- **Keep products away from the treatment area. Dispense pigment and anesthetic before the procedure and then put the containers away**

- Clean floors and walls regularly with a low level disinfectant

- Do not work on clients if you are sick

- Clean up spills immediately

- Clean and decontaminate all surfaces that may have come in contact with pigment/blood/saliva/OPIM thoroughly

- Keep your work tray clean to prevent cross contamination

Clean and disinfect all contact surfaces thoroughly according to disinfectant manufacturer's instructions

Tape a small waste bag to your treatment table/rollabout to help keep your workspace clean

- Make it a rule to de-glove and wash your hands if you need to leave the treatment area for any reason, such as answering the door, taking a phone call, or making a trip to the restroom (in this case you would need to change all of your PPE)

- Use as many disposable items as possible

Disposable pigment ring

- **Use a waste bin with a foot pedal** so that you do not have to touch anything with your hands

- Leave cell phones and cameras outside the treatment area, so that you are forced to de-glove and wash your hands before checking your phone or taking photos

- Never use a staff/kitchen area to prepare your treatment tray. Separate your treatment area from kitchen areas to prevent cross contamination of food and Bloodborne pathogens

- Use barrier film

- If you have an itch, use a cotton swab to scratch your face, not dirty gloves

No food in the procedure area!

Chapter 5 Summary

Chapter 5 Vocabulary:

Hand Sanitizer   Gloves   Lab Coat   Antiseptic
Face Mask   Green Soap   Goggles   Bar Soap
Foaming Soap   Liquid Soap   Plain Soap   Antibacterial Soap
Antimicrobial Soap   Powdered Soap   Cross Contamination
Personal Protective Equipment (PPE)

Chapter 5: Test Your Knowledge Questions

1. What does PPE stand for?

2. You need to put on your PPE in which order?

    a. Gloves, face mask, goggles, labcoat
    b. Labcoat, face mask, gloves, goggles
    c. Labcoat, face mask, goggles, gloves
    d. Goggles, face mask, labcoat, gloves

3. Do you open sterile packaging (for needles, etc) before or after putting on your PPE?

4. Labcoats...

    a. Should have short sleeves
    b. Must be washed every 5 procedures
    c. Are not necessary
    d. Provide protection against splatter

5. Name 3 types of soap. Explain the differences between the 3 you chose.

6. True or False: You can reuse your disposable gloves if you wash them thoroughly and spray them with disinfectant

7. True or False: Gloves must be changed if you leave the treatment area for any reason.

8. Describe how to change your gloves.

9. Goggles and face masks are meant to:

     a. Protect eyes, nose, and mouth from splatter
     b. Help you not breathe on the client
     c. Keep your face clean
     d. None of the above

10. What percentage of bacterial filtration should your face mask have, according to the FDA?

11. True or False: It is perfectly safe to wear flip-flops while working on a client.

12. What is the difference between Standard Precautions and Universal Precautions?

13. What is green soap?

14. True or False: Cleaning the skin with an antiseptic before working is optional.

15. Can you wear rings or bracelets while working? What about underneath your gloves? Why or why not?

16. Is hand sanitizer a substitute for hand washing? Why or why not?

17. Which kind of soap (for hand washing) is best for body art professionals?

     a. Plain soap
     b. Antibacterial soap
     c. Green soap
     d. Antimicrobial soap

18. You can cross contaminate an object by doing all of the following EXCEPT:

     a. Touching a doorknob
     b. Answering your phone
     c. Scratching an itch
     d. Changing your gloves and washing your hands properly

19. List five ways you can prevent cross-contamination

20. True or False: You should treat all blood and bodily fluids as if they are contaminated and dangerous to you.

21. True or False: You do not need to remove jewelry as long as your gloves cover your jewelry.

22. True or False: You should wash your hands before you put on clean gloves.

23. You should never...

    a. Work on clients if you are sick
    b. Save used needles
    c. Save used pigment
    d. You should never do any of the above

24. How long should you wash your hands?

    a. 10 seconds
    b. 20 seconds
    c. 30 seconds
    d. 40 seconds

25. True or False: Cool water tightens your pores and makes it more difficult for pathogens to penetrate your skin

26. True or False: It is important to cover any surfaces you may touch with barrier film.

Chapter 5 Bonus: Identifying Cross Contamination

Can You Find the Cross Contamination Problem With This Picture?

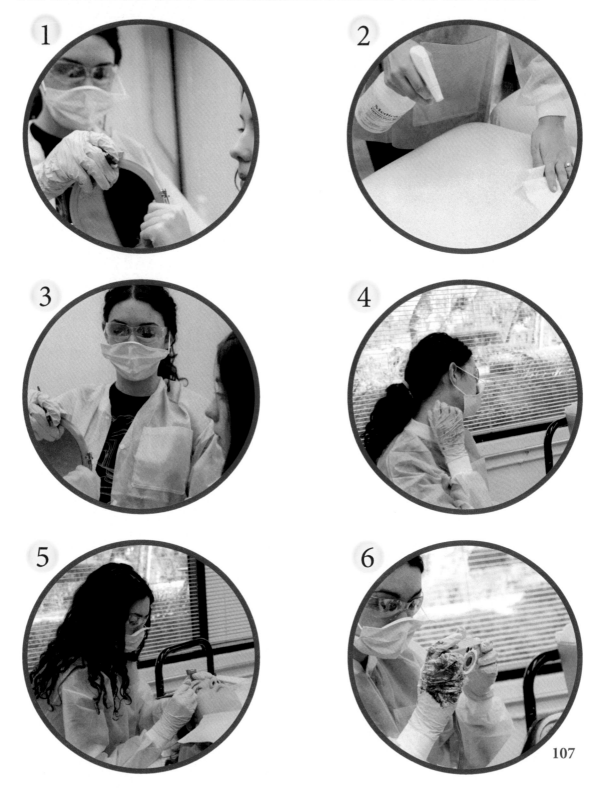

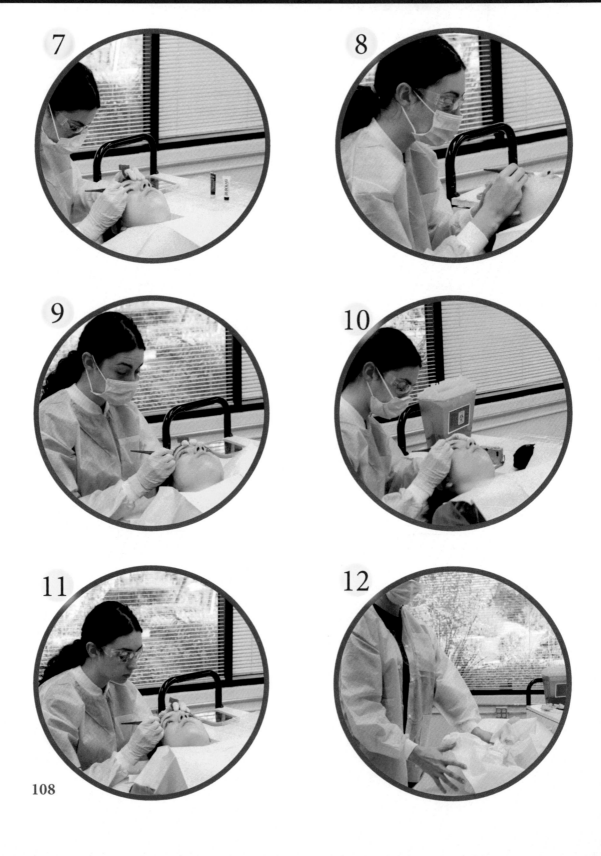

Notes

Notes

Notes

Chapter 6: Occupational Exposure in Body Art

6.1 What is Occupational Exposure?

Learning Objectives for This Chapter:

- Understand what a needle stick is and how to avoid it
- Know what to do if a needle stick occurs
- Know what to do if you are exposed to pigment or blood splatter
- Be able to properly record an incident if one occurs by following an exposure control plan

Occupational Exposure is a term that means you have been exposed to bloodborne pathogens at work. A needle stick (when you accidentally puncture your skin with a contaminated needle) is an example of occupational exposure. A needle stick puts your blood in direct contact with contaminated color and your client's blood. Pigment or blood splatter in your eyes, nose mouth, or open skin is also considered occupational exposure.

6.2 Avoiding Needle Sticks and Splatter During Body Art

Use common sense when handling needles and working on open skin. In addition to standard precautions, practice these habits to avoid exposure to bloodborne pathogens.

- Always point needles away from yourself
- Never bend or tamper with your needles. Contaminated sharps must not be bent, recapped, removed, sheared, or broken
- Put needles down on your tray each time you reach for other items such as gauze, cotton swabs, etc during the procedure. If holding a machine, hold it at a safe distance from yourself and others while wiping, etc
- Never wipe your client's skin with a needle in your hand. Use the other hand if you cannot put the needle down
- Do not attempt to clean your needles with gauze or tissue and your hands. If you want to clean excess ink off of a needle, set gauze on your treatment tray and wipe the needle on the gauze. This keeps your hand away from the sharp end
- Needles should be the first item disposed of immediately after a treatment
- When throwing multiple used needles away in the sharps container, do not pick up a handful of needles, pick them up one at a time

<u>Never save or reuse needles</u>

113

6.3 Exposure: What Should I do if I get a Needle Stick?

1   If the area is bleeding, squeeze it gently until a little blood is released

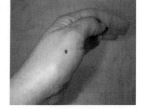

2   Wash the puncture using non-abrasive (so you don't open it further) antimicrobial soap and warm water

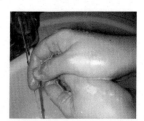

3   Bandage the puncture, and go to the emergency room immediately for testing and shots. If you are an employee, and are exposed to OPIM during a procedure, you have the right to request a vaccine for Hepatitis B within 10 days at your employer's expense, unless you have already been vaccinated against HBV. (According to OSHA standard 1910.1030 (f)(1)(i) and 1910.1030 (f)(1)(ii))

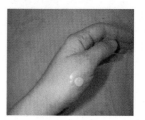

4   You must document the incident. Write down what happened, without any names to keep your personal information private

5   Give your report to your employer to keep on file

Sharps Injury Log

Please Complete the Following:

Date of Incident: _____

Time of Incident: _____

Describe the Incident: _____

_____

_____

_____

_____

_____

What Actions Were Taken at the Hospital?: _____

_____

_____

Hepatitis B Vaccine Needed?_____

Location Where Incident Occurred: _____

Location of Needle Stick on the Body (ex: left wrist): _____

Notes/Recommendations on How to Prevent Future Injury: _____

_____

_____

_____

_____

6.4 Exposure: What Should I do if Splatter gets in my Eyes, Nose, or Mouth?

1 Flush the area thoroughly with water for 15 minutes

Why is pigment splatter important? This is the second biggest risk for body art professionals for the transmission of bloodborne pathogens. As pigment splatters during a procedure, it can come in contact with bodily fluids, including blood, and if it enters your body (eyes, nose, mouth) you are at risk for infection. **Note that if pigment splatters on closed/intact skin, this is not occupational exposure, your skin will protect you.** Simply wash the area thoroughly. Splatter is dangerous when it contacts open skin and enters the body.

2 Go to the emergency room immediately for testing and shots

3 You must document the incident. Write down what happened, without any names to keep your personal information private

4 Give your report to your employer to keep on file

Pigment Splatter Exposure Report

Please Complete the Following:

Date of Incident: _____

Time of Incident: _____

Describe the Incident: _____

_____

_____

_____

_____

_____

What Actions Were Taken at the Hospital?: _____

_____

_____

_____

Location Where Incident Occurred: _____

Location of Pigment Splatter on the Body (ex: right eye): _____

Notes/Recommendations on How to Prevent Future Injury: _____

_____

_____

_____

_____

 **6.5 Post Exposure Follow Up**

Follow up with any testing and/or vaccines performed at the hospital.
Counseling can be provided to the employee at the cost of the employer. The employer is **required** to provide the exposed employee with a copy of any test results within 15 days of receiving them from the hospital or testing lab.

Risk of Infection Following Exposure

Depends on the disease:
- For HIV/AIDS risk of infection by needle stick is less than 1%
- For HIV/AIDS the risk of infection following exposure from pigment splatter is approximately 0.1%
- For Hepatitis B (HBV) the risk of infection by needle stick is approximately 30%
- For Hepatitis C (HCV) the risk of infection by needle stick is less than 2%
- Risk of HBV and HCV from exposure to splatter is unknown

Chapter 6 Summary

Chapter 6 Vocabulary:

Occupational Exposure   Exposure Control Plan
Needle Stick Exposure Report
Pigment Splatter Exposure Report

Chapter 6: Test Your Knowledge Questions

1. What is a needle stick?

    a. The device you put your needle into
    b. When a contaminated needle accidentally punctures your skin
    c. A tattoo needle
    d. None of the above

2. List five ways you can avoid a needle stick.

3. If you get a needle stick you should...

    a. Wash the puncture
    b. Go to the doctor for testing
    c. Document the details of the incident
    d. All of the above

4. What is regulated waste?

5. True or False: Regulated waste can be thrown in the garbage

6. True or False: Contaminated needles are considered regulated waste.

7. What should you do if you get a needle stick? Write down the steps you need to take right afterwards.

8. What should you do if you get pigment/ink splatter in your eyes, nose, or mouth? Write down the steps you need to take right afterwards.

9. Why does a sharps container need to be near the area where you do procedures?

    a. So you don't have to walk very far
    b. So that clients in other areas don't see your needles
    c. It reduces the risk of a needle stick from walking about with a contaminated needle
    d. Sharps containers don't have to be near where you work

10. True or False: If you get blood, pigment splatter, or OPIM on your **intact** skin, is this considered occupational exposure to bloodborne pathogens and you need to go to the hospital for shots and testing.

Notes

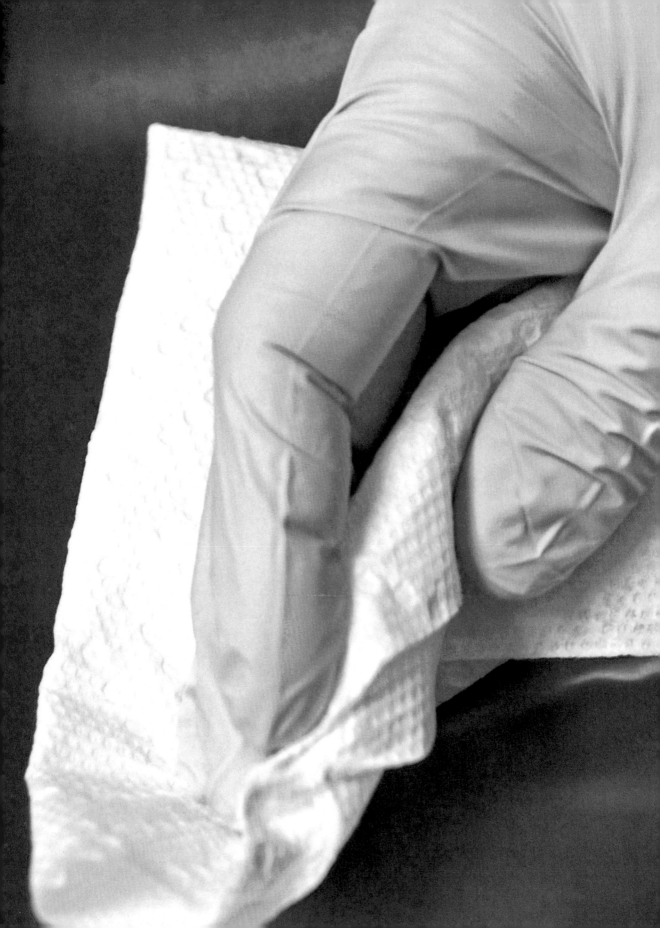

Chapter 7: Cleaning Up: Decontamination, Disinfection, and Sterilization

7.1 Reusable and Non-Reusable Items

Items such as needles, used pigment, client drapes, gauze, and cotton swabs are considered **non-reusable items**. These are things that you throw away when the procedure is finished. **Reusable items** are things you can wash, disinfect, sanitize or sterilize, such as machine parts, tweezers, treatment beds, and mirrors.

What to Do With Reusable Items?

The way you clean any reusable items depends on how the items are used in the first place. We separate reusable items into three categories, **Non-Critical, Semi-Critical, and Critical Items,** depending on the risk of infection when each is used. For example, critical items must be sterilized between uses because they come into direct contact with blood.

Type of Reusable Item	What it Means	Example	What to Do With it
Non-Critical Items	These items are everyday surfaces that may come in contact with intact skin. **There are two categories: clinical contact items and housekeeping items**	**Housekeeping Items**: floors, walls, blinds, etc	Use a low level disinfectant
		Clinical Contact Items: treatment beds and treatment tables you may touch during the procedure	Use an intermediate level disinfectant
Semi-Critical Items	These are items that may come in contact with open (non-intact) skin or mucous membranes such as the eyelids	Tweezers, machine parts, respiratory equipment in hospitals	Sterilize if possible, if not, use a high level disinfectant or disposables
Critical Items	These are items that come into direct contact with blood, such as catheters and implants	Piercing jewelry, tattoo needles, or implants	Most of these items are **single use only**. Dispose of in the sharps container

Reusable Items	Picture	Classification	What to Do
Tweezers		Semi-critical item	Sterilize if possible, if not, use a high level disinfectant or disposables
Metal finger rings for pigment cups		Semi-critical item	Sterilize if possible, if not, use a high level disinfectant or disposables
Plastic or metal autoclavable handles		Semi-critical item	Sterilize if possible, if not, use a high level disinfectant or disposables
Protective eyewear (goggles, eyeglasses, etc)		Semi-critical item if blood or splatter on it, otherwise clinical contact	Use an intermediate level disinfectant, or a high level disinfectant if visibly contaminated with blood or splatter
Magnifiers		Semi-critical item if blood or splatter on it, otherwise clinical contact	Use an intermediate level disinfectant, or a high level disinfectant if visibly contaminated with blood or splatter
Pillows and linens		Clinical contact item	Launder
Labcoats, scrubs, other protective clothing		Semi-critical item if blood or splatter on it, otherwise clinical contact	Discard or launder
Utility gloves for cleaning		Clinical contact item	Use an intermediate level disinfectant

Reusable Items	Picture	Classification	What to Do
Plexiglass/reusable cup holders		Semi-critical item	Sterilize if possible, if not, use a high level disinfectant or disposables
Sterilizable machine parts		Semi-critical item	Sterilize
Non-sterilizable machine parts		Semi-critical item	Use a high level disinfectant
Hand mirrors		Clinical contact item	Use an intermediate level disinfectant
Treatment beds and treatment tables (roll about tables)		Clinical Contact Item	Use an intermediate level disinfectant
Lamps		Clinical Contact Item	Use an intermediate level disinfectant
Metal, glass, and other reusable treatment trays/containers/holders		Clinical Contact Item	Use an intermediate level disinfectant
Non-disposable design tools such as metal rulers, stencils, etc		Clinical Contact Item	Use an intermediate level disinfectant

***Note: Every machine is built differently and parts that are sterilizable may be different between machines. For example, one machine may have a sterilizable tube or casing, while another may not. Follow the manufacturer's instructions for proper cleaning and information on which parts can be safely sterilized.

Non-reusable items	Picture	Classification	What to Do
100% disposable needles		Critical item	Dispose of in the sharps container
Machine needles, disposable machine parts (grommets, tips, tubes, sponges, rubber bands, etc)		Critical item	Dispose of in the sharps container
Face masks		Semi-critical item	Throw away
Gloves		Semi-critical item	Throw away
Gauze		Critical item	Throw away
Cotton swabs		Critical item	Throw away
Tissues		Critical item	Throw away
Paper towels		Clinical contact item	Throw away
Treatment bed paper		Clinical contact item	Throw away
Barrier film		Clinical contact item	Throw away
Pigment/ink cups		Critical item	Throw away
Any brushes		Critical item	Throw away
Disposable plastic treatment trays		Clinical contact item	Throw away
Lip rolls		Critical item	Throw away
Disposable design tools (single use surgical rulers, etc)		Clinical contact item	Throw away

7.2 Decontamination and Disinfection

After each procedure you need to decontaminate and disinfect any surfaces you or your client come in contact with. This includes your treatment table/roll-about where you keep your tray, your treatment bed, your chair, lamp, cords, and protective eyewear (and your eyeglasses and side shields if you use them).

Step 1: Decontamination:

* **<u>Decontamination means to remove germs</u>** either mechanically (with a brush, wipes, or ultrasonic cleaner) or chemically (soap and water)

* The purpose of decontamination is to remove debris, such as hair from tweezers, or dirt/grime from your hands

* Wear gloves and a labcoat while decontaminating dirty items

* If washing in the sink, clean the sink afterwards

* If you are going to sterilize the item, rinse it thoroughly after decontamination, dry it using clean hands, and place it in a sterilization bag to be sterilized later

Other Cleaners

An ultrasonic cleaner, washer-disinfector, or washer-sterilizer will decontaminate instruments for you

Mechanical decontamination of tweezers

What is a Hospital Grade Disinfectant?

Hospital Grade Disinfectants are used in hospitals and other clinical settings such as plastic surgeons offices, veterinary offices, and nursing homes. These disinfectants are known for having the ability to kill three specific pathogens: **pseudomonas, staphylococcus aureus, and salmonella.** You do not need to have a Hospital Grade Disinfectant for body art, just follow the OSHA requirements outlined on the disinfectant page. Disinfectants must be: virucidal, bactericidal, fungicidal, tuberculocidal, kill HBV and HIV, and be registered with EPA.

Disinfectants

Choice, Use, and Storage of Disinfectants

Level of Disinfectant	What it Does	Use it For
Low level disinfectants:	Kill **most** bacteria, fungi, and **some** viruses, but **not** tuberculosis or bacterial spores	routine cleaning of your *non-critical items*: **floors, walls, blinds, curtains, and other surfaces** that may come in contact with intact skin
Intermediate level disinfectants:	Kill **most** bacteria, fungi, tuberculosis, and **most** viruses, but **not** bacterial spores	*Semi-critical items* such as **treatment beds, treatment tables, your chair, eyeglasses, and any lamps**
High level disinfectants:	Kill **all** bacteria, fungi, tuberculosis, viruses, and **some** bacterial spores, borders on rendering items sterile	*Semi-critical items* such as **coil or rotary machine parts that are heat sensitive or cannot be sterilized**

*Non-sterilizable machine parts that are covered in barrier film must always be high level disinfected between clients. Barriers can help prevent cross contamination but are not foolproof.

- Intermediate and high level disinfectants:

    Must be **germicidal** (kills bacteria/germs)

    Must be **fungicidal** (kills fungi)

    Must be **virucidal** (kills viruses, particularly HIV and AIDS viruses)

    Must be **tuberculocidal** (kills TB)

- **Any disinfectant you use must be effective against HIV and HBV**

- Any disinfectants you use must be registered with the **Environmental Protection Agency (EPA).** This means the bottle will have an EPA registration number on the back

- See the EPA website for a list of approved disinfectants and choose the ones you need from there

Step 2: Disinfection:

- **Disinfection means to stop the reproduction of any living germs on an object.** Some disinfectants also kill living germs, however they do not kill spores

- **Will not effectively sterilize objects because disinfectants do not kill all of the spores of microorganisms (spores can only be killed with sterilization)**

- Can be used to clean items that cannot be sterilized, such as countertops and eyeglasses

- Can be used to remove germs on small items before sterilization

- Items to be disinfected must be cleaned first (decontaminated)

Disinfectant Baths

- Disinfectant baths (such as Barbicide®) may be used as long as they are covered to prevent the spread of germs.

- Note that baths do **not** sterilize items

- Disinfectant bath chemicals must completely cover implements and soak for the required amount of time (as stated in the disinfectant's manufacturing instructions, usually about 10 minutes)

- Disinfectant baths must be changed at least once a week or when the solution becomes cloudy

- Always use clean gloves or tongs to remove soaked implements

- Rinse soaked implements with water three times to remove disinfectant (use tongs) and dry thoroughly

Vocabulary

Non-Reusable Items	Environmental Protection Agency (EPA)	
Fungicidal	Decontamination	Virucidal
Low Level Disinfectant	Intermediate Level Disinfectant	Disinfection
Germicidal		

Some pathogens cannot be destroyed with just one pass of spraying and wiping. You need to spray again, and wait a few minutes before you wipe the second time around. The time you need to wait varies depending on which disinfectant you use, so make sure you follow the instructions for your disinfectant. In general, the wait time is 10 minutes for the second pass.

You must also wear your Personal Protective Equipment (PPE) while disinfecting contaminated surfaces in case of accidental cross contamination, or in case the disinfectant you use is harmful to your skin.

1. Spray your disinfectant on a contaminated surface (chair, treatment bed, etc)	
2. Wipe the surface with a clean paper towel & discard the paper towel	
3. Spray the surface again	
4. Leave/wait the time indicated on manufacturer's instructions	
5. Wipe the surface with a new paper towel & discard	

Storing Disinfectants

- Label all of your disinfectant containers

- Try to store disinfectants in their original containers

- Follow manufacturer's instructions for storage. For example, "keep out of reach of children"

- Store disinfectants separate from food, preferably in their own cabinet away from light and heat

- Make sure you can see the disinfectant's expiration date on the label, so that you can replace it when necessary

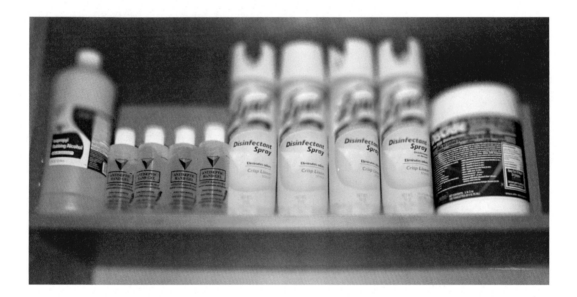

Vocabulary	Reusable Items	High Level Disinfectant	Non-Critical Items
	Tuberculocidal	Semi-Critical Items	Critical Items
	Disinfectant Bath	Hospital Grade Disinfectant	Housekeeping Items
	Clinical Contact Items		

 ## 7.3 Sterilization

- Destroys all germs and their spores with heat, pressure, and/or chemicals, to the extent that there are so few they cannot be detected
- There are four main ways to sterilize: steam autoclave, dry heat, ethylene oxide, and chemical vapor
- Operating sterilizers improperly can cause your instruments to be non-sterile, **always sterilize your items according to the sterilizer manufacturer's instructions**
- Items to be sterilized must be taken apart (if possible), decontaminated, then dried and put in sterilization bags

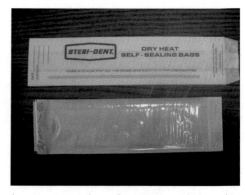

Put decontaminated implements inside sterilization bags

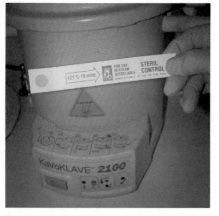

A biological indicator, or "spore strip" used in steam sterilization loads, the yellow dot turns blue when spores are destroyed

- Special biological indicators called **spore strips** are used to show whether an item has been sterilized. Spore strips are strips of paper with a colored dot (with actual spores on the dot) that turn a different color when no spores are present
- One spore strip should be used with each sterilization load to verify that items have been properly sterilized (have killed spores)

A Note on Boiling Water:

Boiling water can kill many types of bacteria and some viruses, which is why it is often used to make water safe to drink. However, **boiling does not sterilize objects** because normal temperatures/times boiled are not high enough to kill spores.

Sterilizer Testing

What is sterilizer testing and why do I need to do it?

Sterilizer testing is used to determine whether or not your sterilizer is working properly. Special testing strips called **indicators** need to be run through your sterilizer once a month and sent to a testing company to check for pathogens. Records of regular testing are a great indication that you have a clean, safe, professional shop. Some states even *require* routine testing, check with your local authorities.

How do I test my sterilizer?

1. Contact a testing company to participate. They will send you a kit to help you get started.
2. Once a month, sterilize an indicator strip from your kit with a normal sterilization load. When the load is finished, *__immediately__* take the strip and mail it to the testing company.
3. The company will check the strip and if it passes the test (i.e., you get a **negative** result) you will receive a record of its passing to keep on file.

If the strip fails the test

(i.e., you get a **positive** result):

- The lab will call you immediately to let you know to stop using the sterilizer and will send you a record to keep on file
- Quarantine (isolate, keep separate) all items sterilized between the time of your last spore strip test and this failed test
- Do not use any items sterilized between the time of your last test and this one until they are re-packed and re-sterilized with a sterilizer that has passed the test. **You can use a back up sterilizer if you have one and it has passed recently**
- Do not use the sterilizer that failed the test until it has been fixed, tested again, and has passed the test

What Can Cause a Failed Test?

- Overloading the sterilizer or using the wrong settings
- Storing test strips improperly
- Clogged drains and vents
- A sterilizer in need of repair

Record Keeping

Sometimes the testing company will give you a certificate to show that you participate in their program. This is a good thing to post in your shop to let others know you test regularly. You also need to keep records of each monthly test report you receive. These are important to have for inspections and to prove that your instruments are sterile, and that your sterilizer is in good working order. Keep records on file according to laws in your state. The average time is 2-3 years.

Chemical Integrators

Chemical Integrators: A chemical integrator gives information on the temperature and time sterilized for steam sterilization. There are six different classes, no one class is "better" than another, they are just different categories. In body art, we typically use Class V integrators when we sterilize instruments.

Chemical integrators typically have a bar that travels across the strip as heat and moisture contact the indicator during the cycle.

Chemical Integrator Class	What it is Used for?
Class I	To show that each **individual** pouch or pack in the load is sterile. Ex: sterilization tape
Class II	**Specialty** tests such as testing for air leaks in a vacuum steam sterilizer
Class III	**Single** variable testing. Ex: testing for the correct temperature **only**
Class IV	**Multi** variable testing. Ex: testing for temperature, time, and concentration
Class V	Testing **all** critical variables during sterilization. This is the most complete test and can sometimes be subsituted for biological indicators
Class VI	Testing all critical variables for a **specific** cycle. Ex: 3 minute cycles or 15 minute cycles

Which Chemical Integrator to Use?

Class V integrators are the easiest and most comprehensive chemical tests available for body art sterilization.

Biological Indicators: A biological indicator contains live spores (spore strip) on a dot that changes color when spores are killed during the sterilization process. Biological indicators are considered the gold standard when testing for sterility.

Should I Use Biological, Chemical, or Both?

There are different requirements for indicators and monitoring depending on your field. Hospitals monitor weekly, with both biological indicators **and** chemical integrators. If you use implants, such as those used for piercing, you must always use at least a biological indicator for every sterilization load. The safest decision is to use both a biological indicator and a Class V chemical integrator when you sterilize, and test monthly. Chemical integrators ensure that heat/time are applied correctly, and biological indicators show spore deaths.

Preparing/Wrapping Items for Sterilization

Q: Why do we wrap things before sterilizing them?

A: Because as soon as you remove the sterile instruments from the machine they become at risk for contamination. Unpackaged items will become unsterile immediately. To keep items sterile, wrap them in bags before sterilizing!

- If you have assembled items such as coil or rotary machines, you need to disassemble them as much as possible. The more simplified/disassembled an item is, the better it will sterilize
- **Items to be sterilized must be clean (washed with soap and water to remove debris) and dry before being placed in sterilization bags**
- <u>Items to be sterilized must be placed in sterilization bags and labeled with the date</u>
- When you package items for sterilization, do so in a clean environment away from sinks used for cleaning and treatment areas, and do so with clean hands

Sterilization Bags

There are many different kinds of bags you can use to pack items for sterilization. Make sure you choose a type of material and package that is approproate for the sterilization method you use. For example, if you use dry heat, be sure to use sterilization bags that can withstand high temperatures, i.e., not plastics that can melt in the sterilizer.

- Use bags that won't tear easily
- Use bags that protect against moisture

Broken Machine Parts?

If part of your machine breaks in a way that it cannot be cleaned and sterilized properly, for example, if pieces become corroded, replace the broken parts! Using and sterilizing damaged equipment is not only bad for your work, it increases the risk of infection from improper cleaning and sterilization.

Four Ways to Sterilize: Steam Autoclave, Dry Heat, Ethylene Oxide, and Chemical Vapor

Steam Autoclave (the most common way to sterilize)

- Steam autoclaves kill living organisms and their spores with high temperatures, time, pressure, and moisture. Water is heated in an inner bath in the autoclave machine until it forms steam, which rises and fills every small space with heat and pressure to kill bacteria and spores

- Steam autoclaves are usually the least expensive and most efficient way to sterilize

- Steam autoclaves must be registered with the Food and Drug Administration (FDA) This means that the model you buy is approved by the FDA and effectively sterilizes objects you put in it. Ask to see the registration number on the packaging before you buy one
- Steam autoclaves are the <u>only</u> approved sterilization equipment in California for body artists

Pros	Cons
Economical: $200 and up to buy	Steam can eventually corrode instruments, causing deformities in plastics and rusting in metal
Fast: takes 8-10 minutes to sterilize items (this varies between models)	You need to buy distilled water often to refill the machine
Reliable, lasts about 10-15 years	
Easy to use	

What Could Cause a Steam Autoclave to Fail a Sterilizer Test?

A steam autoclave

136

- Not preheating the sterilizer

- Interrupting the cycle

- Not sterilizing the right amount of time

- Using the wrong temperature and/or pressure settings

- Overloading the chamber

- Bad gaskets, clogged drains, filters, or vents

- Leaving sterilized items in the chamber and allowing them to get wet, which compromises the packages, spore strips, and instruments inside

Dry Heat

- Dry Heat Sterilizers render objects sterile when used between 250°F (very slow to sterilize, several hours) and 340°F (much faster, 1-2 hours). These sterilizers use oven-like heat to kill germs
- Dry Heat Sterilizers must be registered with the Food and Drug Administration (FDA) This means that the model you buy is approved by the FDA and effectively sterilizes objects placed inside. Ask to see the registration number on the packaging before you buy one

Pros	Cons
Fairly economical: $500 and up to buy	Using high heat can melt plastic instruments, crack mirrors, burn paper, and eventually ruin metal items from constantly reheating to sterilize
Using **low** but adequate heat and long sterilization time will prolong the life of your instruments because there is no steam to corrode them	High heat will burn sterilization bags, you need special nylon bags for dry heat sterilizers, fortunately these are about the same price
Reliable	Slow, 30 mins and up (this varies between models) per cycle. Faster units are available but are very expensive
Easy to use	

A dry heat sterilizer

What Could Cause a Dry Heat Sterilizer to Fail the Sterilizer Test?

- Not preheating the sterilizer

- Interrupting the cycle

- Not sterilizing the right amount of time

- Using the wrong temperature settings

- Overloading the chamber

Note: A regular household oven is NOT the same as a dry heat sterilizer and cannot be used to sterilize implements

Ethylene Oxide (EtO)

- Ethylene Oxide (EtO) gas sterilization kills all germs and their spores with temperature, humidity, and time exposed to the gas
- Due to expensive equipment and strict requirements by the **O**ccupational **S**afety and **H**ealth **A**dministration (**OSHA**) requirements, EtO is usually only found in hospitals and commercial areas
- EtO is ideal for delicate instruments that would otherwise be damaged by sterilization

Pros	Cons
Will not corrode, melt, crack or burn any instruments	Expensive, the long sterilization time means you must have a large inventory in order to work while items are processing
Low temperature (86-140°F) you can sterilize your goggles, magnifiers, or other items that would melt in an autoclave	**Strict OSHA requirements**
Will not dull delicate edges, such as tweezer points	Slow: 4 hours and up per cycle (this varies between models)
	Gas refills and sterilization bags are expensive
	Implements must be dry before sterilization, EtO reacts with water to form residue which can be dangerous
	<u>**EtO gas is extremely dangerous**</u> **to humans in the case of accidental exposure**

What Could Cause EtO to Fail the Spore Strip Test?

- Interrupting the cycle

- Not sterilizing the right amount of time

- Using the wrong temperature settings

- Overloading the chamber

- Not following manufacturer's instructions

Chemical Vapor

- Heats cleaning chemicals under pressure (270°F and 20 psi) without corroding instruments
- The cleaning agents used (mainly formaldehyde, alcohol, and water) are often **carcinogenic** (cancer causing) and require adequate ventilation in the room to use
- Takes about 20 minutes per cycle (this varies between models)

Pros	Cons
Economical: $200 and up	Needs a well ventilated area so you do not expose yourself to chemical vapors
Fast: takes 20 minutes to sterilize items (this varies between models)	Chemicals are expensive and need to be replaced often
Good for heat sensitive items and items easily damaged by steam	Strict OSHA requirements
	Chemical vapors used in these machines carcinogenic and unsafe for humans
	Used chemicals have special disposal requirements, you cannot just throw them away

What Could Cause Chemical Vapor to Fail the Spore Strip Test?

- Not drying instruments before using

- Interrupting the cycle

- Not sterilizing the right amount of time

- Using the wrong temperature settings

- Using wrong amounts of chemicals

- Using poor quality chemicals

- Overloading the chamber

So Which Method is Best?

Steam autoclaving is currently the most common form of sterilization in small practices and salons, <u>however</u> the method with which you choose to sterilize depends completely on you. Some professionals like the low maintenance and affordability of dry heat, while others find that their equipment is so delicate that EtO gas is the only option for them. There is no single method better than the others. The choice depends on your own circumstances, the equipment you use, and how often you sterilize. Some professionals do not need a sterilizer at all, if they use 100% disposable items, such as presterilized piercing needles.

Here are some questions to help you decide which method is best for you:

- Do you have back-to-back appointments and need to sterilize items quickly? If yes, you should consider fast methods, such as an autoclave or chemical vapor

- Do you need to sterilize the same items over and over? Are these items expensive and delicate? If yes, consider a method that will not corrode your instruments, such as chemical vapor, low heat dry heat, or an EtO gas machine

- Do you work in a hospital or other location that processes many tools? If yes, you may have access to an EtO gas sterilizer or be able to meet the OSHA requirements to use one

- Are you patient enough to wait for longer methods? Do you have a large enough inventory to keep working while items are sterilizing? If yes, consider dry heat or EtO gas sterilization

- Do you have the resources to maintain the unit you choose? Meaning do you have time to change the water in your autoclave, or buy more refills for your chemical vapor or EtO gas machine? If you are very low maintenance, or do not need to sterilize often, dry heat may be the best option for you

How to Decontaminate Tools and Surfaces With Household Bleach
A 1/4 cup of bleach mixed into 1 gallon of water provides a strong enough solution to effectively decontaminate most tools (before sterilization) when soap and clean water is not available. While wearing gloves, mix the solution, allow to stand for 30 minutes, then soak your implements for 10 minutes to decontaminate. Do not use for electrical components or cords, wipe these down with a damp paper towel soaked in the solution instead. Make sure to label the container so others know to keep it away from children and pets!

7.4 After you Sterilize: Storing Sterile Items

You can leave sterile items in the sterilization bags you used for the machine, as long as you follow these rules:

- The type of package/bag you use determines how long you can store the item, read the bag/package manufacturer's instructions for how long you can store items inside
- Write down the date you sterilized the item on the bag
- Write down the expiration date on the bag (for example, if the instructions the bag came with say that the bag is good for 1 year, write down the expiration date as one year following the sterilization date)
- **Never** open a bag to use the instrument and then tape it back up again, this does not make the package "good as new"
- Keep sterile items and the spore strip used with them in a clean, dry, rigid (puncture proof), covered container
- Store at room temperature and low humidity (35-50%) so that bags do not get wet or damp
- The storage area must be clean and dry
- Keep sterile items away from any dirty supplies and keep off of the floor
- Handle sterile items as little as possible

The reason items do not stay sterile forever is that eventually bacteria will break into the sterilization bag and reproduce. While the item may still appear clean and safe to use, after the storage time has elapsed items are no longer sterile.

Here are some ways to check if an item is sterile:

- Check to see if the seal is still in place, if the item is even partially open, it is not sterile
- Check to see if the package is free of dust, tears, dirt, or dampness
- Check the spore strip in your container, is it the right color? (according to manufacturer's instuctions)

Clean Up Checklist

In this order:

1. **Throw away your used needles in the sharps container**
2. **Properly dispose of any regulated waste**
3. **Throw away any excess pigment/ink and pigment/ink cup used**
4. Throw away used disposables (gauze, cotton swabs, tissues etc)
5. If you taped a waste bag to your table to prevent cross contamination, use the tape to close the waste bag, and discard in the trash
6. Throw away your treatment tray (if using disposable treatment trays)
7. If using a reusable items such as stainless steel trays, tweezers, machine parts, etc. place in a closed, labeled container and move to the decontamination area (your cleaning sink) for cleaning later
8. Remove barrier film
9. Take off your gloves carefully without touching your skin with the dirty gloves, and throw away in the garbage
10. Remove and dispose of your face mask
11. Remove your protective eyewear for disinfecting or washing
12. Remove your labcoat carefully so you do not cross contaminate, turn it inside out, and throw it in the dirty laundry bin
13. Wash your hands
14. Take any after pictures, give client aftercare instructions/ointment to take home, conclude appointment
15. Wash your hands again
16. Put on a new pair of gloves
17. Disinfect all surfaces. Spray, wipe, spray, wait 10 minutes, then wipe again
18. De-glove and wash your hands! All done! From here you can begin decontaminating any reusable instruments (at your separate cleaning sink) and begin preparing them for disinfection or sterilization

Chapter 7 Summary

Chapter 7 Vocabulary:

Non-Reusable Items   Disinfection   Fungicidal   Reusable Items
Decontamination   Germicidal   Virucidal   Tuberculocidal
Low Level Disinfectant   Sterilization   Spore Strip   Chemical Vapor
High Level Disinfectant   Non-Critical Items   Critical Items Dry Heat
Disinfectant Bath   Semi-Critical Items   Steam Autoclave
Hospital Grade Disinfectant Sterilizer Testing   Ethylene Oxide (EtO)
Housekeeping Items   Biological Indicator
Clinical Contact Items   Chemical Indicator
Environmental Protection Agency (EPA)
Intermediate Level Disinfectant
Class I-VI Chemical Indicators

Chapter 7: Test Your Knowledge Questions

1. What does asepsis mean?

    a. Clean
    b. Dirty
    c. Old
    d. New

2. True or False: Metal tweezers are a reusable item.

3. What is the difference between decontamination and disinfection?

4. True or False: Your disinfectant does not need to be on the EPA's list of approved disinfectants.

5. What is the Spray-Wipe-Spray Technique?

6. Sterilization...

    a. Removes debris only
    b. Kills bacteria but not their spores
    c. Can be achieved by putting objects in boiling water
    d. Destroys all germs and their spores

7. All of the following are ways to sterilize an object except:

>   a. Dry heat
>   b. Disinfectant spray
>   c. Ethylene Oxide gas
>   d. Steam autoclave
>   e. Chemical vapor

8. True or False: Steam autoclave takes the most amount of time to sterilize an object.

9. Which method of sterilization will not melt, corrode, or damage the items being sterilized?

>   a. Dry heat
>   b. Ethylene Oxide gas
>   c. Steam autoclave
>   d. Chemical vapor

10. Sterilized items can be stored...

>   a. In plastic bags for up to one year
>   b. Up until the time indicated on the bag's instructions
>   c. In plastic or paper bags for up to two years
>   d. Indefinitely

11. True or False: You may use plastic wrap as barrier film.

12. True or False: Non-critical items need to be high level disinfected

13. What is the difference between a biological indicator and a chemical indicator?

14. High level disinfectant is used for:

>   a. Clinical contact items
>   b. Housekeeping items
>   c. Machine needles
>   d. Machine parts that cannot be sterilized

15. What is the difference between a Critical Item and a Semi-Critical Item?

16. List three ways a sterilizer can fail a test.

17. Which class of chemical indicator is best for testing sterilizers in body art?

18. What is a Hospital Grade Disinfectant?

19. True or False: You can use a low level disinfectant for your floors and walls.

20. Your disinfectants must all be:

   a. Registered with the EPA
   b. Able to destroy HIV and HBV
   c. Properly labeled
   d. All of the above
   e. None of the above

21. True or False: Ethlyene Oxide is a good way to sterilize instruments that would otherwise be damaged in a steam, dry heat, or chemical vapor sterilizer.

22. True or False: A steam sterilizer does not need to be registered with the FDA.

23. Does boiling water sterilize items? Why or why not?

24. Critical items:

   a. Come into direct contact with blood
   b. Include tattoo needles and piercing needles
   c. Are usually single use items
   d. All of the above

Notes

Notes

Chapter 8: Forms for Body Art

8.1 Which Forms Do I Need?

- Infection Control Plan
- Release Form for clients
- Infection Report for clients
- Pre and Post Treatment Instructions
- Sterilization Log
- Sterilization Test Log/Certificate
- Used Implements Log
- Exposure Incident Reports (for accidents, such as needle sticks or pigment splatter exposure)

8.2 What is an Infection Control Plan? Why Do I Need One?

An Infection Control Plan (ICP) is a written set of rules and plans on how to prevent injuries and infection at your facility. Every facility or business that anticipates contact with blood or bodily fluids is required to have an infection control plan. A thorough, specific plan will do the following:

- **State which risks are present at your facility**
  - Ex: "Employees may be exposed to small amounts of blood and/or saliva while working at this facility"
- **State your plan to control these risks**
  - Ex: "This facility uses Standard Precautions to minimize the risk of exposure to bloodborne pathogens"
- **Engineering Controls**
  - State how new equipment, placement of sharps containers, etc is determined
  - Show where sterile instruments, disinfectants, antiseptics are stored

- Outline where decontamination, disinfection, and/or sterilization of instruments takes place
- Show how containers are labeled. Ex: "Containers are labeled with the purchase date, expiration date, child warning label, and contents."

- **Work Practice Controls**
  - How to set up and clean up the treatment area
  - Show the types of PPE you use at your facility, state the order to don them, and how they are removed, disposed of, or cleaned
  - Outline how your facility disposes of sharps
  - How to decontaminate, disinfect, and sterilize the treatment areas and/or implements
- **Housekeeping**
  - Outline how often surfaces are cleaned, the specific disinfectants used, laundry procedures, etc
- **Steps to Take if Exposure Occurs**
  - Give exact directions
  - Outline whose responsibility it is to arrange an HBV vaccine and specific steps for that person to take. Ex: "Linda will call the hospital at this number ###-###-#### to arrange an HBV vaccine for any exposed personnel at the time of exposure."
  - Post exposure follow up instructions
- **Record Keeping**
  - State how and where you keep important records, such as sterilization logs, used needle logs, client release forms, etc

 8.3 Sample Infection Control Plan

The following pages contain a sample ICP to help you create your own.

Sample Infection Control Plan

<u>**Body Art Facility Name**</u>
Infection Prevention And Control Plan
Operation Procedures

This policy was written to comply with the requirements of the California Safe Body Art Act Section 119313. Infection Prevention and Control Plan as well as OSHA 29 CFR 1910.1030 and 29 CFR 1910.1200.

Employee Duties:

_____ is responsible for maintaining this ICP and ensuring it is up to date with all current procedures.

_____ will maintain and provide all necessary personal protective equipment (PPE), engineering controls (e.g., sharps containers)

_____ will ensure that adequate supplies of the aforementioned equipment are available at all times.

_____ will be responsible for keeping employee training current as required by OSHA, and to keep records of training (certificates).

_____ will be responsible for record keeping for this facility.

List of Employees at Risk of Exposure to Bloodborne Pathogens:

Technician/Artist Name:_____

Technician Address:_____

_____

_____

Phone Number: _____

Driver's License #:_____

State:_____ Date of Birth:_____

Technician/Artist Name:_____

Technician Address:_____

_____

_____

Phone Number: _____

Driver's License #:_____

State:_____ Date of Birth:_____

Sample Infection Control Plan

List of Employees at Risk of Exposure to Bloodborne Pathogens:

Technician/Artist Name:_____

Technician Address:_____

_____

_____

Phone Number: _____

Driver's License #:_____

State:_____ Date of Birth:_____

Technician/Artist Name:_____

Technician Address:_____

_____

_____

Phone Number: _____

Driver's License #:_____

State:_____ Date of Birth:_____

Technician/Artist Name:_____

Technician Address:_____

_____

_____

Phone Number: _____

Driver's License #:_____

State:_____ Date of Birth:_____

Technician/Artist Name:_____

Technician Address:_____

_____

_____

Phone Number: _____

Driver's License #:_____

State:_____ Date of Birth:_____

Sample Infection Control Plan

1.   **Work Practice Controls: Set Up and Tear Down Procedures for Workspaces/ Stations**

   a.   **Set Up**
      i.   Disinfect the procedure area if any activity has taken place between tear down/clean up of the last client and this client.
      ii. Place barriers on counters or work surfaces, drawer handles, lamps, etc., using clean hands
      iii. Gather supplies in client's presence, then in this order:
         1.   Seat the client on treatment bed after all paperwork has been filled out and before photos have been taken
         2.   Wash hands up to elbows for a minimum of 30 seconds
         3.   Put on labcoat
         4.   Put on face mask
         5.   Put on protective eyewear
         6.   Put on gloves
         7.   Drape the client
         8.   Cleanse the client's skin
         9.   Begin procedure

      iv. Any time the artist leaves the procedure area gloves must be removed, thrown away, and the hand washing process must be completed again. New gloves are required before reentering the treatment zone

   b.   **Tear Down**
      i.   Cleanse client's skin with gentle/nonirritating soap and water. Apply ointment and clean dressing (if using).
      ii. Give client aftercare instructions.
      iii. Remove and dispose of gloves. Wash hands for a minimum of 30 seconds and put on new gloves.
      iv. Place needles in sharps container, one at a time, pointing away from oneself
      v.   Remove barrier film and throw in trash.
      vi. Remove any waste bags, used gauze, tissues, cotton swabs, etc., and throw in trash
      vii. Spray work surface with disinfectant and wipe down according to section 4 below
      viii. Wash hands with soap and water.

In preparing inks, dyes or pigments to be used by an artist, only commercially available single-use or

Sample Infection Control Plan

individual portions of dyes or pigments in clean, single-use containers shall be used for each client. After the tattoo procedure, the remaining unused dye or pigment in the single-use individual containers shall be discarded along with the container.

2.   Work Practice Controls: Procedures to Prevent Cross Contamination of Instruments and Work Site During Procedure

Cross contamination issues will be discussed with all body art technicians working at this facility. Here is an example of

Some Examples Of How This Can Occur Are As Follows:
- If one or more artists share the same equipment, such as machines, tables, trays, etc.
- If used/dirty instruments/surfaces and clean instruments/surfaces come into contact with one another.
- If clean instruments are placed on unclean surfaces.
- If strict artist hygiene is not observed.(Continued):
- If contaminated dressings, spatulas, disposable gloves are not disposed of immediately and appropriately after use.
- If structural facilities, furnishings and fittings of the premises are not adequately protected, or if surfaces are not thoroughly cleaned between clients.
- If towels and other articles used on clients are not changed or thoroughly cleaned between clients.

Artists should be aware of the potential for unprotected surfaces and equipment to become contaminated with blood and serum during body art procedures.

Some Examples of how This Can Occur are as Follows:

- Adjusting overhead/treatment lamps/fittings.
- Adjusting settings on power packs.
- Answering telephones or cell phones.
- Touching ink/pigment containers or ink trays/pigment cups.
- Touching curtains, drapes, or bin lids.
- Adjusting furniture and equipment. Clients, artists and many others can be at risk if cross-contamination occurs.
- Touching hair, skin or clothes with contaminated gloves

3.   Safe Handling and Disposal of Sharps Waste

Body art studio operators/artists/practitioners shall dispose of waste products in the following manner:

Sample Infection Control Plan

- Needles, razors or other sharp instruments used for patient care procedures shall be segregated from other wastes and placed in sharps containers immediately after use
- Containers of sharp wastes shall be sent to a facility to be managed as a medical waste. Used sharps for this facility shall be sealed and mailed to: _____
- Other disposable waste shall be placed in a trash container lined with a plastic trash bag.
- Waste containers shall be kept closed when not in use.
- Disposable waste shall be handled, stored, and disposed of to minimize direct exposure of personnel to waste materials.

4.   Decontaminating and Disinfecting Environmental Surfaces

- Any implements that do not come in contact with non-intact skin or mucosal surfaces shall be washed with soap and water and a brush small enough to clean interior surfaces.
- The surfaces of all worktables and chairs or benches shall be constructed of materials that are smooth, nonabsorbent and easily decontaminated.
- Work tables/trays and chairs or benches shall be decontaminated with a germicidal solution after each body art application. Hard surface disinfection will consist of using _____. All hard surfaces in the procedure area will be disinfected after each client. The chairs, counters, etc. will be sprayed with _____. The disinfectant will be allowed a contact time of _____ (according to manufacturer's directions for dilution and contact time), and then wiped down with a paper towel and disposed of in the trash. A second spray and wipe shall be performed according to manufacturer's instructions.
- If the procedure area has been used for any activity between clients it shall be disinfected again.

5.   Decontaminating, Packaging, Sterilizing, and Storing Reusable Instruments

- Body Artists shall use only individually packaged, sterile needles and instruments for each patron/client.
- Clean instruments and sterile instrument packs shall be placed in clean, dry, labeled containers or stored in a labeled cabinet to protect from dust and moisture.
- Each sterile instrument pack shall be evaluated at the time of storage and before use. If the integrity of the pack is compromised the pack shall be discarded or reprocessed before use.

Sample Infection Control Plan

IMPORTANT! Include either section i or ii on this page, (or both!) depending on what you use!

i. This facility uses 100% disposable needles. Records are kept with lot number, expiration date, client name, procedure date, and name of technician with client files/forms. Purchase records for sterile implements will be kept for 90 days and are available if needed.

ii. This facility uses instruments that require sterilization before reuse:

1. Reusable instruments will be disassembled as much as possible before preparing for sterilization to ensure thorough decontamination, disinfection, and sterilization.
2. All reusable instruments shall be decontaminated (at a sink separate from any hand washing sinks), disinfected, and then allowed to dry before packaging for sterilization.
3. Instruments to be sterilized shall be clean and dry, and then packaged in sterilization bags labeled with the date.
4. Sterilization is accomplished by this method (circle one): steam, dry heat, ethylene oxide gas, chemical vapor, other.
5. Sterilizer testing is accomplished by this method:_____
6. Test records are available for ____ years from test date
7. This facility uses (circle one or write in another method below): biological indicators, chemical indicators:_____
8. Sterile items/instrument packs are stored in a clean, dry place, separate from cleaning areas, kitchen areas, and work spaces As the owner of this facility, I maintain the responsibility to educate my employees once every two years on bloodborne pathogens as required by OSHA. I will provide PPE and HBV vaccinations for my employees as needed. I certify that the information in this Exposure Control Plan is true and up to date each year:

Owner Name_____

Title _____

Signature: _____

Date: _____

Print Name (Witness):_____

Signature:_____

Date: _____

8.4 Release Forms, Including Pre and Post Treatment Instructions, and Incident Reports

A great release form will let your clients know exactly what they are getting into. State every risk, no matter how unlikely, that may occur, and have your client understand these risks. Release forms should also have a list of contraindications for the body art you perform. These may vary depending on the procedure. The example in the following pages is for permanent makeup procedures as well as tattooing.

In general, release forms should include:

- Your client's name, address, phone number
- Your client's emergency contact information (name, address, phone number)
- **A description of the procedure**
- **What to expect from the procedure**, including suggested care and any medical complications that may arise as a result of the procedure
- A list of **contraindications** for your procedure. This will vary depending on your procedure and what is required in your state. For example, in California it is illegal to tattoo a minor. However, in Michigan, it is allowed as long as parental/guardian consent is given
- **A statement regarding the permanent nature of body art.** For example: "I understand that tattoos are permanent."
- **A list of statements regarding the risks** involved with your procedure, and a signature that acknowledges all risks
- A statement regarding the regulatory status of tattoo inks/pigments. For example, "Tattoo inks and pigments are not regulated by the FDA."
- **An option to take or waive a 6 week color patch test for tattoos and permanent makeup**
- An **attached infection/incident report** in case of infection
- A copy of **attached pre and post treatment instructions** for the client to read before the procedure, which include care instructions, restrictions on activities such as bathing, recreational water activities, gardening, and contact with animals, information on when to seek medical attention, and symptoms of infection
- A record of the **artist's name, contact information, driver's license #, and birthday**
- **A record of the colors and tools/needles used, lot #, expiration date, and procedure performed with any notes**
- **A place or separate form to record any touchups** with colors and needles used, and artist's information, as updated. Also have the client rerelease you and update any changes to medical history

Sample Release Form
for Tattoo Procedures
Consent And Release Agreement For Body Art

Name of Releasor
(client):_____

Who resides at
(street
address)_____
(city)_____(zip)_____(phone)(_____)_____-_____(alt.
phone)(_____)_____-_____

Please list your Emergency Contact Below:
Name: _____
Who resides at
(street
address)_____
(city)_____(zip)_____(phone)(_____)_____-_____(alt.
phone)(_____)_____-_____

Agreement

1. **Description Of The Procedure**

    A. This procedure will implant permanent color/designs to the desired area using pre-sterilized needles attached to a coil machine.

2. **What To Expect From This Procedure**

    A. There may be minor swelling and or irritation following this procedure. With proper care, healing should take place within 5-10 days, depending on the individual. See below for risks, the possibility of medical complications, and post treatment instructions.

3. **Acknowledgement Of The Risks Or Complications Associated With The Body Art Procedure.**

    A. The Releasor has been informed by the Releasee of the possible dangers that may occur as a result of having a tattoo procedure performed. The Releasor acknowledges that those dangers may include allergies from ink used in the procedure(s), fever blisters or cold sores from lip procedures, swelling, bruising (although rare), temporary minor bleeding, redness or pinkness, and soreness. **The Releasor understands and acknowledges that the tattoo procedure may permanently alter the appearance**

Sample Release Form
for Tattoo Procedures

of the Releasor's skin, which may or may not be desirable to
the Releasor.

B.   Now, the Releasor having been fully and completely advised
of all inherent risks, dangers, and complications which may
arise from a tattoo procedure, voluntarily assumes all and any
risks, dangers, or complications which may arise as a result of a
tattoo procedure.

To help minimize any risks, the Releasor will answer Yes or No
the following conditions in order to describe if the Releasor
has any of the following medical conditions:

IF YES, EXPLAIN

1. Keloid   Yes   No
Location: _____

2. Diabetes   Yes   No

_____

3. Alcoholic   Yes   No

_____

4. Epilepsy   Yes   No

_____

5. Under 18 yrs. Old   Yes   No
If yes, the client must wait until at least 18 years of age to have a tattoo, or obtain
parent/guardian written consent

6. Using Accutane   Yes   No

_____

7. Using Retin-A   Yes   No

_____

8. Hemophiliac or other bleeding disorder   Yes   No

_____

9. Pregnant or nursing   Yes   No
If yes, then you are cannot receive a tattoo at this time.

10. Active Skin Disease   Yes   No

_____

Sample Release Form
for Tattoo Procedures

11. Autoimmune Disorders   Yes   No

12. Hepatitis   Yes   No

13. Blood Disease   Yes   No

14. Cold Sores   Yes   No

15. Herpes   Yes   No

16. Cancer   Yes   No

17. Tuberculosis   Yes   No

18. Steroids   Yes   No

19. Chemical Peel   Yes   No

20. Using Glycolic Acid   Yes   No

21. Other Tattoos   Yes   No

22. Heart Condition   Yes   No

23. Allergies to ANY of the following:
medications or topical salves such as Bacitracin, Lanolin, Lidocane, Novacaine, Metals, Neosporine, Paba, Rubber Gloves, Latex, Lidocaine, Epinephrine, Tetracaine, Benzocaine? Are you allergic to any Antibiotics?   Yes   No

24. History of Medication Use?   Yes   No
If yes, please list_____

25. Taking Medication Now? Including prescribed antibiotics prior to dental or surgical procedures? Any supplements?
    Yes   No
If yes, please list_____

26. Any other Diseases   Yes   No

Sample Release Form
for Tattoo Procedures

27. Taking Blood Thinners Such as Aspirin, Coumadin, or Ibuprofen?

    Yes   No

28. Any surgeries?   Yes   No

29. Currently under doctors care?   Yes   No

30. Optical Herpes   Yes   No
    If yes, then you cannot receive permanent eyeliner or tattoos near the eyes.
31. Mitral Valve Prolapse   Yes   No

32. Cardiac Valve Disease   Yes   No
    If yes, then you are cannot receive a tattoo

4.   Patch Test Waiver
            I agree to (initial one):

_____ **Waive patch test** and I agree to release the owner of this establishment, assistants, artists, and ink/pigment manufacturer(s) from any and all liability related to allergic reaction or any other reaction to applied pigments/inks.

_____ **Take a 6-week patch test** prior to the tattoo procedure. I agree to release the owner of this establishment, assistants, artists, and ink/pigment manufacturer(s) from any and all liability related to allergic reaction or any other reaction to applied inks/pigments.

A.   The Releasor agrees to accept full responsibility for the COLOR, AND DESIGNS of each and every tattoo I request.

B.   The Releasor agrees that in the event of a controversy between the Releasor and the Releasee involving a claim in court, the parties shall resolve their dispute through small claims court.

C.   The Releasor agrees that in the event that the Releasor prevails in a judgement against the Releasee, the Releasor agrees that the Releasor will not be entitled to a settlement that exceeds the amount paid for the work accomplished by the Releasee.

Sample Release Form
for Tattoo Procedures

D. The Releasor acknowledges receipt of pre-procedure information and post-treatment care instructions, has read them, has been verbally told them, understands them, and agrees to adhere to them in order to help prevent infection.

E. The Releasor understands that follow up procedures/appointments may be required

5. **Consent To Tattoo Procedure**
The Releasor fully and voluntarily consents to have the release perform the tattoo procedure(s) and is fully aware and informed of all and any inherent risks, dangers, and complications that may occur as a result of the procedure(s) as described in this agreement. The Releasee has reviewed the medical history of the Releasor and has answered all of the Releasor's questions satisfactorily.

6. **Release Of All Claims**
A. In order for the Releasee to perform any tattoo on the Releasor for which the Releasee is volunteering to have performed after having been fully informed of all dangers and risks involved as described in this agreement including but not limited to: swelling, allergy to pigment, pain, infection, redness, soreness, eye injury, and itching.

I_____, voluntarily request that the Releasee perform such procedure(s) and I, for myself, my respective heirs, assigns, administrators, personal representatives, and next of kin, hereby will forever release and hold harmless the Releasee, management, their affiliates, officers, members, agents, employees, other participants, and sponsoring agencies from and against any and all claims, damages, or liabilities that may result from the permanent cosmetic procedure(s) as described in this agreement including costs of medical care that may arise from the procedure including post-op care. The Releasor acknowledges that no other claims or guarantees have been made by the Releasee other than is expressly written in the agreement.

Signature of Releasor _____Date_____

Signature of Releasee (witness)_____ Date _____

Sample Release Form
for Tattoo Procedures

Recitals

a.   The Releasor wishes to have the tattoo procedure(s) performed by the Releasee.

b.   The Releasor has been informed by the Releasee that color/ink/pigment will be implanted into the skin and as a result the skin color will be permanently altered.

c.   The Releasor has been informed by the Releasee that there is pain involved in the procedure(s).

d.   The Releasor has been informed by the Releasee that there may be adverse side effects such as swelling, bruising (extremely rare), temporary minor bleeding, redness or pinkness, and soreness.

e.   The Releasor has been informed by the Releasee that there will be some fading of the color. The Releasee has made no guarantees or promises to the Releasor as to how much color will be retained or how the color will fade. Color may have to be reapplied to the desired area before satisfaction of the desired color is obtained The Releasor has been informed by the Releasee that there will be a minimal charge for each reapplication of the color.

f.   The Releasor has been informed by the Releasee that ink may migrate or spread to an undesired area.

g.   The Releasor has been informed by the Releasee that lips may feel dry and tight after the lip procedure.

h.   The Releasor has been informed by the Releasee that eye injury may occur from the cosmetic eyeliner tattoo procedure.

i.   In the event of a diagnosed allergic reaction, the Releasor agrees to have a punch biopsy in order to determine certainty regarding the cause.

j.   The Releasor has been informed by the Releasee that an infection may occur, and that post-op procedure care instructions will have to be followed in order to help prevent this from occurring.

k.   The Releasor has been informed by the Releasee that an allergic reaction may occur from the ink/pigment used in the tattoo procedure.

l.   The Releasor has been informed by the Releasee that ink/pigment may be accidentally misplaced which may result in a permanent disfigurement.

m.   The Releasor has been informed by the Releasee that fever blisters or cold sores may occur after lip procedures, if the Releasor is prone to having them. The Releasor has been informed by the Releasee to obtain an appropriate oral prescription and take as prescribed in order to help minimize an outbreak of fever blisters.

Sample Release Form
for Tattoo Procedures

n. The Releasor has been informed by the Releasee not to take any aspirin or Ibuprofen before the tattoo procedure as it may promote bleeding.

o. The Releasor has been informed by the Releasee that a low-level magnet may be required if the Releasor is ever scanned by an MRI (Magnetic Resonance Imaging) machine because pigments used in the procedure(s) may contain inert oxides. The Releasor agrees to inform the MRI technician of these circumstances. 1 out of 1000 people may be sensitive to any MRI. Further information is available at www.MRIsafety.com.

p. The Releasor has been informed by the Releasee to wait one year after a tattoo procedure before donating blood.

q. The Releasor has been informed by the Releasee to use sunscreen on a daily basis because constant exposure of the tattoo to the sun may fade the color or even cause irritation to the skin.

r. The Releasor has been informed by the Releasee that any effective removal method of tattoo may result in scarring and/or a permanent disfigurement.

s. The Releasor has been informed that some pigments contain titanium dioxide and that under a laser, this substance can crystallize and turn black.

t. The Releasor has been told that an allergic reaction can be triggered when needles enter into previously tattooed work involving ink of unknown origins, resulting in oozing, redness, and itching which may have to be excised or lasered in order to calm down the allergy.

The Releasor, having read and been verbally told of all of the above Recitals by the Releasee, nevertheless, desires to have the tattoo procedure(s) performed by the Releasee and is willing to enter into this agreement. The Releasor has been given an opportunity to ask questions about the procedures and the implements to be used and the risks and hazards involved and believes that he/she has sufficient information to give this informed consent.

I have read, been verbally told, and understand each of the above recitals

_____   _____
(customer signature)   (date)

Photographer's Model Release

I consent to have my picture taken by the Releasee for Before and After photos, record-keeping purposes, and any portfolio related work/work-ups as the Releasee sees fit.

_____   _____
(customer signature)   (date)

Sample Release Form
for Tattoo Procedures

Procedure Information (Office Use Only)

Technician/Artist Name:_____

Technician Address:_____

_____

_____

Phone Number: _____

Driver's License #:_____

State:_____ Date of Birth:_____

Color(s), Anesthetic, or formula
(swab some actual color in the circle.
List anesthetic and date if used)

Date Used, Lot # and Exp Date

_____

Location(s):_____

Comments:

Needles Used,

Date Used, Lot # and Exp Date

_____

Comments:

Sample Release Form
for Tattoo Touchups

Client Retouch/Touchup Consent Form

Has your medical history/medications changed since your last appointment on _____? (circle one)

        Yes   No

If yes, please list any changes below: _____

_____
_____
_____
_____
_____
_____
_____
_____
_____
_____
_____
_____
_____
_____
_____
_____
_____

I certify that the above information is true and correct. I consent to have the tattoo procedure touchup.

_____   _____
(customer signature)   (date)

Sample Pre and
Post Treatment Instructions
Pre And Post Treatment Instructions

Pre-Treatment Instructions For All Procedures:
1. Do not take any aspirin within 5-7 days before the procedure as it promotes bleeding. Tylenol or other non-aspirin pain relievers may be taken I hour prior to procedure.
2. If you are having lip procedures done and have had previous problems with cold sores, fever blisters, or mouth ulcers, the procedure is likely to re-activate the problem. Take a preventative medication two weeks prior to the procedure to help prevent cold sores.
3. We recommend allergy testing of pigment before the planned procedure.
4. Do not drink alcohol before the procedure. It promotes bleeding and increases your sensitivity.

Post Treatment Instructions For All Procedures:

1. Apply antibiotic ointment sparingly twice a day for seven days following the procedure, using a clean cotton swab; not your fingertips. If you experience sensitivity to the ointment or allergic reaction, stop use immediately and switch to plain Vaseline. Seek medical care if necessary.
2. We recommend that ice packs be applied for 10-15 minutes each hour for the first 24 hours following the procedure, except at bedtime. It is important to place clean tissue paper between the ice bag and the skin to prevent frostbite. The ice is used to minimize swelling and provide comfort. After the first 24 hours the use of ice is no longer beneficial. Do not take aspirin, as this promotes bleeding. Tylenol ™ is recommended for temporary pain relief.
3. Most normal activities can be resumed immediately. We would recommend that heavy exercise such as aerobic dancing, weight lifting, etc. be delayed for approximately 2-3 days following the procedure.
4. Avoid all washing and contact with water (including recreational water sports and pools for 24 hours following the procedure. After 24 hours you may gently clean the procedure area with a mild soap and water as needed. Baths, showers, swimming, and other recreational water activities are then permitted as long as the procedure site does not become wet. After two weeks or after the pigment scabs over (whichever comes first), you may resume all normal methods of swimming and bathing.
5. Stay out of the sun! If you must be out and about, wear a hat and lots of sunscreen.
6. If you are a blood donor you cannot give blood for 1 year following the procedure (American Red Cross)
7. Avoid gardening and contact with animals for two weeks following the procedure to prevent infection.
8. Do not under any circumstances perform invasive skin treatments such as

Sample Pre and Post Treatment Instructions

microdermabrasion, chemical peels, microcurrent facials, laser, botox, restylane/lip fillers,injections, implants, piercings etc until the procedure has fully healed and the skin is back to normal.

9. Symptoms of infection may or may not occur. They include: "redness, swelling, tenderness of procedure site, red streaks going from procedure site towards the heart, elevated body temperature, or purulent drainage from procedure site." (stated as required from California's Safe Body Art Act: AB300 Article 2, 119303 C)

10. If you experience symptoms of infection (listed above) or allergic reaction, seek medical care immediately

11. Fading or loss of pigment may occur. Some flaking off of the pigment may occur on some skin types. Do not be alarmed. It is normal. There should be pigment under the skin where the pigment has flaked off. If there is no pigment there, then a touch up will be required.

12. Judgment of your final results should be deferred until one month following the procedure. If you have any further questions or concerns please contact our office.

8.5 Injuries, Accidents, and Infection Reports

In case of an accident leading to exposure (a needle stick or pigment splatter):

1 If the area is bleeding, squeeze it gently until a little blood is released

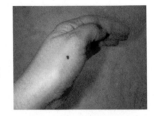

2 Wash the puncture using non-abrasive (so you don't open it further) antimicrobial soap and warm water

3 Bandage the puncture, and go to the emergency room immediately for testing and shots. If you are an employee, and are exposed to OPIM during a procedure, you have the right to request a vaccine for Hepatitis B within 10 days at your employer's expense, unless you have already been vaccinated against HBV. (According to OSHA standard 1910.1030 (f)(1)(i) and 1910.1030 (f)(1)(ii))

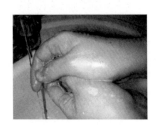

4 You must document the incident. Write down what happened, without any names to keep your personal information private

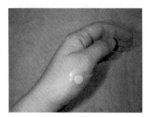

5 Give your report to your employer to keep on file

A client just called me and says that they got an infection, what should I do?

In the case of an infection, fill out the following form and send to your local health department immediately.
Have the client seek medical attention immediately.

Sharps Injury Log

Please Complete the Following:

Date of Incident: _____

Time of Incident: _____

Describe the Incident: _____

_____

_____

_____

_____

_____

What Actions Were Taken at the Hospital?: _____

_____

_____

Hepatitis B Vaccine Needed?_____

Location Where Incident Occurred: _____

Location of Needle Stick on the Body (ex: left wrist): _____

Notes/Recommendations on How to Prevent Future Injury: _____

_____

_____

_____

_____

Pigment Splatter Exposure Report

Please Complete the Following:

Date of Incident: _____

Time of Incident: _____

Describe the Incident: _____

_____

_____

_____

_____

_____

What Actions Were Taken at the Hospital?: _____

_____

_____

_____

Location Where Incident Occurred: _____

Location of Pigment Splatter on the Body (ex: right eye): _____

Notes/Recommendations on How to Prevent Future Injury: _____

_____

_____

_____

_____

Infection, Adverse Reaction, Allergic Reaction Incident Report

To Be Forwarded Within 5 Days of Incident to:

Telephone:

Date Reported:_____

Date of Procedure:_____

Date Mailed to CCEH:_____

Client Name: _____

Address: _____

_____

_____

Work Phone: _____

Home Phone: _____

Color(s) Used:_____

_____

Description of
problem:_____

_____

_____

_____

_____

_____

_____

_____

_____

_____

Attending Physician:_____

Address: _____

_____

_____

Phone: _____

8.6 Sterilization Logs, Sterilization Test Logs, and Used Implement Logs

- Some states require logs of all sterilization loads, sterilization testing, and even procedures and implement logs!
- Check with your local authorities to find out which documents you need to keep on file and for how long

Sterilization and Sterilization Test Logs

What is a **Sterilization Log**? Why do you need it?
- Sterilization logs keep track of when and how you sterilize items. This is important because it proves that:
    1. You sterilized the items before using them on clients
    2. You sterilized items properly

To do this: write down the date sterilized, time, temperature, pressure, and/or other details of the sterilization process in a log

Sterilization Test Log? What is that?
Some states require that you routinely test your sterilizer for effectiveness. The test log is the certificate your testing company issues you each time testing has been completed.
- Keeping sterilizer test logs (if you test your sterilizer) is important because:
    1. It shows you routinely test your sterilizer
    2. It shows that your sterilizer is working properly

To do this: keep the certificate the testing company gave you on file

Used Implement Logs

What is a **used implement log**? Why do you need it?

- These logs keep track of when you use needles, and the clients who had those needles applied to their skin. This is important because it shows:
    1. When and who needles were used on
    2. Which needle size, lot number, and expiration was used
    3. In case of an infection or adverse reaction, you can pinpoint the exact needle to determine whether it had any effect on the situation

    To do this: write down the needle size used, lot number, expiration date, date used, time, client name, and artist name

- This information should be on your client's release forms anyway, but if needed you can easily create this log for your local authorities

Other Record Keeping: Do I Need to Keep Injury Reports on File?

If you have an injury in the workplace and if you have 10 or less employees (including temporary employees), you do not need to make or keep any records for workplace injuries according to OSHA regulation 29 CFR part 1904.

In addition, the body art industry (under "Miscellaneous Personal Services") beauty industry, barber industry, and clinics of medical doctors are **exempt** from keeping injury records according to OSHA regulation 1904 Subpart B Appendix A.

<u>Two Exceptions:</u>
- If OSHA or the Bureau of Labor Statistics (BLS) sends you a survey letter asking about workplace injuries. If you receive this letter, first of all do **not** panic! The government randomly sends these requests to gather information on workplace injuries for public information. Visit **www.BLS.gov** to see some examples of the reports they create. If you receive this letter, follow the instructions and keep any injury records for the year following the letter. Once the year is over, send in your report, and you're finished!
- No matter the size, industry, or injury, if a workplace incident/accident kills any employee, or if three or more employees are sent to the hospital, you must report that incident to OSHA. Obviously this is highly unlikely! However if you ever need to report this kind of incident the forms you would need are on OSHA's website: www.osha.gov

Sample Sterilization Log

Date and Time	Employee Name	Item Sterilized	Temperature	Pressure	Time/ Duration of Cycle

Sample Sterilization Test Log

Certificate of Participation

Body Art Studio Name

This certifies that Body Art Studio _____ has successfully participated in the sterilization monitoring service provided by _____ testing company. This facility uses sterilization equipment that is routinely monitored for sterility assurance. The results of our test indicate that this facility's instruments have been adequately sterilized for the period of _____ to _____. This service is recommended by the American Dental Association (ADA), the Centers for Disease Control (CDC), and the Occupational Safety and Health Administration (OSHA).

Program Valid Through: _____

_____

Signature of Testing Company Representative

Sample Used Implements Log

Date and Time	Artist Name	Client Name	Needle Size/ Type Used	Lot Number	Expiration Date

8.7 Record Keeping: How Long to Keep/Maintain Records?

Records should be well organized and available to local authorities when requested.

- Exposure Control Plan: Update every year or as changes occur, keep forever

- Release Form for clients: Update every year or as changes occur, keep forever

- Infection Report for clients: Keep with the client's release form, keep forever

- Sterilization Log: Log every cycle, filing time varies by state

- Sterilization Test Log/Certificate: Log every month, filing time varies by state

- Used Implements Log: Log every used item, filing time varies by state

- Exposure Incident Reports (for accidents, such as needle sticks or pigment splatter exposure): Keep throughout the duration of employment, +30 years, remember to keep all related documents with the report such as test results, healthcare professional's opinion, etc.

- Records of Employee Training: Keep for 3 years on file

8.8 Hepatitis B Vaccination Requirements for Employers

If you are an employer, you have a responsibility to:

- Provide an HBV vaccine free of charge after OSHA Bloodborne pathogens training has been completed

- Provide the vaccine within 10 days of initial employment unless the employee has already received the vaccine, is proved immune to HBV, or declines the vaccine

- Note: If the employee initially declines, and later decides to have the vaccine performed, you must provide the vaccine at that time

- Ensure that vaccines are given at a time and place reasonable to your employees

- Ensure that vaccines are performed by or under the supervision of a licensed physician or under the supervision of another licensed healthcare professional

- Ensure that vaccines are provided according to recommendations of the U.S. Public Health Service

- Ensure that all tests related to HBV vaccines are provided free of charge, and all tests performed at an accredited laboratory

- The opposite page has a release form for your employees should they decline vaccination. Keep this on file for the duration of employment.

HBV Vaccine Declination Form

I understand that due to my occupational exposure to blood or other potentially infectious materials I may be at risk of acquiring hepatitis B virus (HBV) infection. I have been given the opportunity to be vaccinated with hepatitis B vaccine, at no charge to myself. However, I decline hepatitis B vaccination at this time. I understand that by declining this vaccine, I continue to be at risk of acquiring hepatitis B, a serious disease. If in the future I continue to have occupational exposure to blood or other potentially infectious materials and I want to be vaccinated with hepatitis B vaccine, I can receive the vaccination series at no charge to me.

_____

(printed employee name)

_____   _____

(employee signature)   (date)

[56 FR 64004, Dec. 06, 1991, as amended at 57 FR 12717, April 13, 1992; 57 FR 29206, July 1, 1992; 61 FR 5507, Feb. 13, 1996]

8.9 Employee Training Requirements for Employers

Trainers have a responsibility to:

- Provide adequate occupational exposure training free of charge upon employment, during working hours, and ensure that employees participate in the training program
- Provide annual training
- Provide additional training as new procedures and/or equipment are introduced
- Provide training that is comprehendable/easy to understand for employees

Chapter 8 Summary

Chapter 8 Vocabulary:

Exposure Control Plan	Pre and Post Treatment Instructions
Contraindications	Infection Report
Sterilization Log	Sterilization Test Log
Used Implement Log	Release Form
Exposure Incident Report (Sharps Injury or Pigment Splatter)	

Chapter 8: Test Your Knowledge Questions

1. What is an Exposure Control Plan?

2. Your Pre and Post Treatment Instructions:

    a. Must be given to the client before the procedure
    b. Must be given to the client after the procedure
    c. Must be posted in your office
    d. None of the above

3. True or False: Requirements for forms such as Pre and Post Treatment Instructions are the same in every state.

4. Why do we keep sterilization/used needle logs?

    a. To comply with government regulations
    b. To track how and when items are used and sterilized
    c. To provide proof that items used in facilities are sterile
    d. All of the above

5. True or False: A Used Implement Log is required in **every** state.

6. True or False: You can decline a Hepatitis B vaccine before becoming a tattoo artist

7. Are client release forms confidential? Why or why not?

8. As an employer, how many days do you have to give your employee the results of a test following an exposure incident?

    a. 5
    b. 10
    c. 15
    d. 30

9. How often do employees in a body art facility need to be trained in Bloodborne pathogens?

    a. Every year
    b. Once every two years
    c. Once every five years
    d. One time only

10. How long does an employer have to keep employee training records on file?

    a. 1 year
    b. 2 years
    c. 3 years
    d. 5 years

11. True or False: An employer must provide a Hepatitis B vaccine for **free** for all employees who could be exposed to bloodborne pathogens.

12. If a client calls and reports an infection, what should you do?

    a. Hang up
    b. Tell them to seek medical attention immediately, while you fill out an infection report
    and send it in to your local health department (if required in your state)
    c. Tell them to put some rubbing alcohol on it
    d. Have them come in to your office to take a look at it

Notes

Notes

Chapter 1: Test Your Knowledge

1. Pathogens
2. Viruses, bacteria, fungi, protozoa
3. Cocci, baccilli, spirilla
4. False, an example of an incurable virus is AIDS
5. A poison that disrupts bodily functions
6. False, non-pathogenic bacteria are non-harmful
7. C
8. Sterilization
9. B
10. Microscopic animals that reproduce by changing shape and then dividing in half
11. Malaria is spread by mosquitos, this kind of transmission is called vector transmission
12. Fungal spores are the offspring of fungi are created as a means of reproduction; bacterial spores (or endospores) are bacteria that have formed a tough outer coating in order to protect themselves from harsh conditions
13. The destruction of all microorganisms on an object, both pathogenic and non-pathogenic
14.

Autoclaves:	250-270°F and 15-30 psi
Dry Heat:	250-340°F (Temperatures close to 250°F require longer cycle time)
Chemical Vapor:	270°F and 20 psi
Ethylene Oxide:	86-140°F

15. Bacteria's ability to adapt quickly and become resistant to antibiotics; as weaker bacteria are destroyed by the medicine, the stronger, more resistant strains survive and reproduce
16. Alexander Fleming
17. D
18. Create a cool, dry, clean environment
19. An animal, insect, or person that carries and transmits an infection
20. Endogenous, exogenous, nosocomial, and opportunistic
21. If a sick person with an already weakened immune system goes to the hospital and gets HAP from the air, they would have an infection that was from outside the body, from a hospital, and was opportunistic, since they already had a weakened immune system!

Answers to Test Your Knowledge Questions

Chapter 1: Bonus

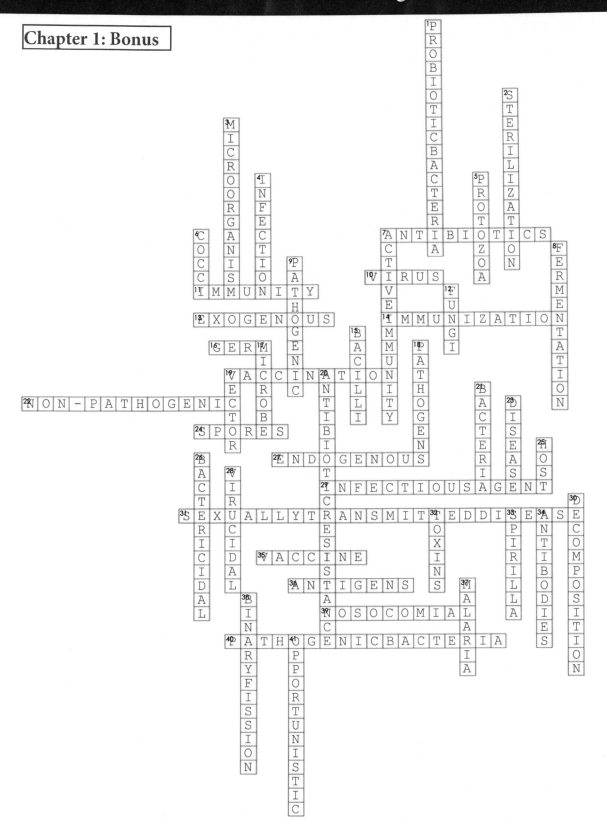

Across and Down answers:

1. PROBIOTICBACTERIA
2. STERILIZATION
3. MICROORGANISM
4. INFECTION
5. PROTOZOA
6. COCC
7. ANTIBIOTICS
8. FERMENTATION
9. PATHOGENIC
10. VIRUS
11. IMMUNITY
12. FUNGI
13. EXOGENOUS
14. IMMUNIZATION
15. BACILLI
16. GERM
17. MICROBE
18. PATHOGENS
19. VACCINATION
20. ANTIBIOTIC
21. BACTERIA
22. NON-PATHOGENIC
23. DISEASE
24. SPORES
25. HOST
26. BACTERICIDAL
27. ENDOGENOUS
28. VIRUCIDAL
29. INFECTIOUSAGENT
30. DECOMPOSITION
31. SEXUALLYTRANSMITTEDDISEASE
32. TOXINS
33. SPIRILLA
34. ANTIBODIES
35. VACCINE
36. ANTIGENS
37. MALARIA
38. BINARYFISSION
39. NOSOCOMIAL
40. PATHOGENICBACTERIA
41. OPPORTUNISTIC

Answers to Test Your Knowledge Questions

Chapter 2: Test Your Knowledge

1. A
2. Infectious Agent, Reservoir, Portal of Exit, Means of Transmission, Portal of Entry, Susceptible Host
3. True
4. D
5. True
6. Other Potentially Infectious Materials
7. Goggles or eye shields, and face masks
8. Saliva
9. False, infectious agents can also enter a new host through any opening in the body, such as the eyes, nose or mouth
10. The last link in the Chain of Infection, which cannot resist the pathogen and becomes infected. Examples: a person or an animal
11. A
12. False
13. D
14. False
15. A
16. A
17. False, symptoms are apparent, but not yet specific
18. The peak of infection, where symptoms are specific and at their strongest
19. True
20. C

Chapter 2: Bonus

Infectious Agent- Reservoir
Clean regularly
(Floors, cabinets, restrooms, sinks, tables)
Disinfect surfaces (Treatment table, beds, counters)
Sterilize instruments (Tweezers, autoclavable tools, etc)

Reservoir-Portal of Exit

Maintain good hygiene (keep food, drinks, and pets away)
Change your labcoat, gloves, masks, and eyewear when they get dirty

Portal of Exit-Means of Transmission

Wipe away any bleeding
Cover your mouth and nose when coughing or sneezing

Means of Transmission-Portal of Entry

Wash your hands
Always wear a labcoat, gloves, face mask, and eyewear
Practice asepsis
Properly dispose of contaminated objects

Portal of Entry-Susceptible Host

Dispose of used needles in the sharps container
Maintain good habits to prevent cross contamination

Susceptible Host-Infectious Agent

Don't work on susceptible clients (pregnant/nursing women, clients with weak immune systems due to medication/disease, see contraindications section
Maintain your health (bolster a strong immune system with good nutrition, exercise, and healthy skin)

Chapter 3: Test Your Knowledge

1. D
2. False, the chances of contracting HIV/AIDS from a needle stick are low
3. A
4. True
5. B
6. TB is an infection of the lungs, and is spread through the air via coughs, sneezes, and saliva
7. False, the disinfectant must be registered with the Environmental Protection Agency (EPA) as tuberculocidal (TB killing)
8. False, they are the same infection
9. True
10. C
11. Double dipping, gardening, contact with pets
12. True
13. Occupational Safety and Health Administration
14. C
15. Liver
16. C

Chapter 4: Test Your Knowledge

1. C
2. True
3. E
4. False
5. F
6. Clinical contact surface is one you might touch during a procedure, an example would be your treatment table or rollabout cart. A housekeeping surface would be your floors, walls, and waiting chairs
7. True
8. False, you should still cover pillows, ink splatter can cause cross contamination

Chapter 5: Test Your Knowledge

1. Personal Protective Equipment (PPE)
2. C
3. After
4. D
5. Green soap is a vegetable based tattooist's soap, powder soap is used to clean tough stains abrasively, antimicrobial soap is effective against most pathogens

6. False, never reuse gloves, except utility gloves, which are only used for cleaning and disinfecting
7. True
8. For examples, see the section on "How to Change Your Gloves"
9. A
10. 95%
11. False, flip-flops do not protect your feet from spills or needle sticks
12. Standard precautions treat all blood and bodily fluids (even if they do not contain blood) as if they are contaminated and dangerous. Universal precautions treat blood and objects visibly contaminated with blood as dangerous.
13. Tattooist's soap, a mild antimicrobial agent used for general cleaning in body art
14. False
15. No, these items can harbor bacteria and tear your gloves
16. No, you must still wash your hands if they are visibly soiled
17. D
18. D
19. Use barrier film, wear PPE, wash your hands, change gloves when leaving the treatment area, clean up spills immediately
20. True
21. False
22. True
23. D
24. C
25. True
26. True

Chapter 5: Bonus

1. Touching a mirror with a glove on, and holding a needle
2. Disinfecting without gloves
3. Open labcoat
4. Scratching with a dirty glove
5. Long hair not tied back
6. Taking photos with dirty gloves
7. Bottles on the table
8. No gloves
9. No goggles
10. Sharps container and camera on the table
11. No face mask
12. Throwing away trash without gloves on

Chapter 6: Test Your Knowledge

1. B

2. See section on "How to Avoid a Needle Stick" examples include: Always point needles away from yourself, never bend or tamper with your needles, never wipe a client's skin with a needle in your hand, do not attempt to clean needles, and be careful while assembling needles

3. D

4. Items are considered regulated waste if you can squeeze a drop of blood or OPIM from them, if caked blood can release a powder when handled, or contaminated needles

5. False, waste must be placed in a leak-proof red bag or container and labeled as regulated waste, then shipped to a medical waste disposal center

6. True

7. See section 6.3 Exposure: What Should I do if I get a Needle Stick?

8. See 6.4 Exposure: What Should I do if Splatter gets in my Eyes, Nose, or Mouth?

9. C

10. False

Chapter 7: Test Your Knowledge

1. A

2. True

3. Decontamination removes germs and debris while disinfectant kills bacteria, but not their spores

4. False, the disinfectant you use must be registered with the Environmental Protection Agency (EPA)

5. This technique is used to intermediate level disinfect surfaces for body art, see chapter 7 for details

6. D

7. B

8. False, steam autoclaves take the least amount of time to sterilize.

9. B

10. B

11. False

12. False

13. A biological indicator shows when spores have been destroyed, while a chemical indicator confirms settings on the sterilizer such as temperature, time, pressure, etc

14. D

15. Critical items come into direct contact with blood (piercing jewelry), while semi-critical items may come in contact with non intact skin (your machine), it is a less direct contact situation

16. Overloading, not following instructions, faulty sterilizer

17. Both biological and chemical
18. HGDs are required to kill 3 specific pathogens: pseudomonas, staphylococcus aureus, and salmonella
19. True
20. D
21. True
22. False
23. No, under average circumstances boiling will not kill spores
24. D

Chapter 8: Test Your Knowledge

1. This is your body art facility's active plan to work at preventing infection, minimizing exposure, and preventing accidents at work. See Chapter 8 for details
2. A
3. False
4. D
5. False
6. True
7. Yes, clients often share confidential medical information on release forms; it is your duty to keep that information private
8. B
9. A
10. C
11. True
12. B

Glossary

Active Immunity- resistance/immunity to a disease given by vaccination.

Acute Stage- The acute stage is the 3rd stage of infection. In this stage the body is showing symptoms unique to the infection it has contracted, and infection is at its peak.

Acquired Immune Deficiency Syndrome (AIDS)- AIDS is the disease that HIV develops into over a period of incubation varying between patients. AIDS weakens the body's immune system, making it extremely susceptible to infection. Even minor infections can pose danger to a patient with full blown AIDS.

Antibacterial Soap- soap that kills bacteria

Antibiotics-a drug that either kills or prevents the growth and reproduction of bacteria, depending on the drug. Certain antibiotics are effective against fungi, protozoa, and bacteria, but none are effective against viruses.

Antibiotic Resistance- when bacteria can grow resistant to antibiotics over generations and time

Antibodies- proteins that help destroy pathogens in the human body.

Antigens- chemical signals that the human body uses to find and destroy pathogens.

Antimicrobial Soap- soap that kills a broad spectrum of germs, including bacteria, viruses, fungi, and protozoa

Antiseptic- a soap or formula used to cleanse the skin of all microbes before a procedure

Asepsis- Asepsis means the lack of infectious agents and pathogenic bacteria. In other words, a clean environment. To practice asepsis means to maintain a clean environment by decontaminating, disinfecting, sanitizing, and sterilizing dirty implements regularly.

Bacilli- rod shaped bacteria

Bacteria-Single celled, microscopic organisms that live in soft tissues, such as the lining of your stomach. Bacteria have a wide variety of functions, from helping break 194 down waste in the body to playing major roles in infections such as tuberculosis.

Bactericidal- having the ability to destroy bacteria.**Bar Soap**- traditional bar of soap used to remove germs with handwashing. Acceptable for home use, but not for body art as wet soap can harbor bacteria.

Binary Fission- the reproductive process of bacteria. Bacteria grow until they are twice their size and then split into two daughter cells.

Biological Indicator- a test strip used to determine the effectiveness of a sterilizer. Biological indicators have live spores on colored dots that change color when spores are destroyed.

Center for Disease Control (CDC)- the CDC provides information to the public on diseases and disease prevention in the United States and throughout the world. The CDC is a great resource for information spanning from proper handwashing to the prevention of emerging diseases. Their website is www.cdc.gov

Chain of Infection- the chain of infection is the pathway an infectious agent takes to infect a new host. There are six links in the chain: the Infectious Agent, Reservoir, Portal of Exit, Means of Transmission, Portal of Entry, and the Susceptible Host. You can cut the chain at any time by practicing asepsis.

Chemical Indicator- gives specific information, such as temperature and time sterilized for steam sterilization. There are 6 classes of chemical indicators.

Chemical Vapor Sterilization- Heats solutions of formaldehyde, water, and alcohol to sterilize instruments

Class I-VI Indicators- Classes of chemical indicators used to test sterilizers in different ways, based on their functions/uses in the workplace. See Chapter 7 for details on each class.

Clinical Contact Items- items that may be touched secondarily during a procedure, such as a treatment tray, rollabout table, treatment bed, or lamp.

Cocci- ball-shaped bacteria

Coinfection- a coinfection is dependent on the existence of another infection. It can occur at the same time as another infection, or at a later time, but it cannot happen by itself.

Contraindications- risk factors that increase the difficulty or ban the possibility of a procedure. Contraindications will vary for different procedures.**Convalescent Stage-** Convalescence means "healing," this is the last stage of infection, where the victim heals and returns to normal.

Critical Items- items that come into direct contact with blood, such as catheters, implants, and body art tools such as tattoo needles and piercing jewelry

Cross Contamination- When germs "cross over" from a contaminated implement to a clean one.

Declining Stage- The 4th stage of infection, when symptoms begin to subside.

Decomposition- the act of bacteria or fungi consuming/breaking down waste into simpler liquids and gases. Decomposition gives rotting garbage its unique smell.

Decontamination- the removal of germs/infectious agents from a contaminated object. This can take place with physical scrubbing, chemically with soap and water, or both at once.

Disease- the harmful effects caused by infection inflicted on the host

Disinfection- kills germs/infectious agents on a contaminated object, usually with a special cleaning spray or disinfectant bath. Disinfection kills bacteria, but not their spores.

Disinfectant Bath- a solution of strong chemicals used as a soak for disinfecting implements before sterilization.

Double Dipping- This is a term that refers to you or your client applying post treatment ointment (such as RecoverAll$_{TM}$) to open skin with a cotton swab, and then touching the contaminated end of that same cotton swab back to the clean ointment. This action increases risk of infection at the treatment site.

Dry Heat Sterilization- a device that kills microorganisms with oven-like heat

Glossary

Emerging Disease- a disease which is either brand new or beginning to infect more of the population than it did previously.

Endogenous Infection- an infection that emerges from inside the body (endo means "inside") such as AIDS, cancer, or diabetes.

Environmental Protection Agency (EPA)- the EPA regulates products such as cleaning chemicals and waste in order to better protect the environment. They also have standards for disinfectants and sterilization. Their website is www.epa.gov

Ethylene Oxide Sterilization (EtO)- a form of sterilization that uses poisonous ethylene oxide gas to sterilize implements at room temperature without damaging intricate parts. See Chapter 7 for more information.

Exogenous Infection- an infection that emerges from outside the body (exo means "outside") such as the common cold, the flu, and tetanus.

Exposure Control Plan- a form/instruction manual written by the body art facility/ staff that outlines procedures/plans for avoiding infection in all daily procedures and tasks of a body art facility. Required in some states. See Chapter 8 for an example.

Face Mask- a disposable mask used to protect the lower half of your face, including your nose and mouth, from pigment splatter during a procedure.

Fermentation- the process by which microorganisms partially eat/consume a substance and change its qualities, whether that be taste, smell, cooking time, or nutrition.

Foaming Soap- liquid soap that foams when pumped from a dispenser. Dispenses adequate amounts of soap in a clean fashion.

Fungi- fungi are yeasts and molds. They like to grow and multiply in warm, moist areas. One example of a fungal infection is athlete's foot.

Fungicidal- having the ability to kill fungi

Germ- an infectious agent. Also sometimes called a microbe or pathogen.

Germicidal- having the ability to destroy a broad spectrum of germs/infectious agents

Gloves- the PPE responsible for protecting your hands.

Goggles- eye protection from splatter during a procedure. Be sure to use goggles that protect from side splatter as well as frontal splatter.

Green Soap- also called "tattooist's soap" this is a mixture of vegetable based soap and water with a medium (about 30%) amount of ethyl alcohol. It is used as an antiseptic and a gentle cleanser for fresh tattoos.

Hand Sanitizer- an antiseptic used to adequately clean hands that are not visibly contaminated with dirt.

Hepatitis- a viral disease that affects the liver.

Hepatitis B (HBV)- a form of Hepatitis, which is a disease that affects the liver. HBV poses a high risk to body art professionals.

Hepatitis C (HCV)- an emerging form of Hepatitis, which is a disease that affects the liver. HCV poses a low risk to body art professionals.

Herpes Simplex Type 1(HSV-1)- a skin infection that causes open sores or lesions on the lips and around the mouth. It can be transmitted through contact such as sharing a drink with an infected person, kissing, sharing lipsticks, and/or sharing toothbrushes or eating utensils.

High Level Disinfectant- a disinfectant that kills all bacteria, fungi, tuberculosis, viruses, and some bacterial spores, borders on rendering items sterile. Use for semi-critical items.

Hospital Grade Disinfectant- a disinfectant used in hospitals and other healthcare settings known for having the ability to kill three specific pathogens: psuedomonas, staphylococcus aureus, and salmonella.

Host- any living plant, animal, or human being that houses an infection

Housekeeping Items- floors, walls, blinds, etc of the workplace. Clean with a low level disinfectant.

Human Immunodeficiency Virus (HIV)- the virus that is the precursor to AIDS. A victim may have no symptoms for years before developing AIDS.

Immunity- having a resistance or protection from disease

Incubation Stage- the first stage of infection, the victim shows no symptoms yet but still carries the infection.

Infection- the implantation and reproduction of a disease causing microorganism on top of or inside of the tissues of a host.**Infection Report**- a form attached to client releases in case of infection, to be filled out if an infection occurs and sent to the local health department. Required in some states, see Chapter 8 for an example.

Infectious Agent- a form of bacteria, fungi, a virus, or protozoa that can potentially infect a host. The first link in the chain of infection.

Intermediate Level Disinfectant- a disinfectant that kills most bacteria, fungi, tuberculosis, and most viruses, but not bacterial spores. Used for cleaning semi-critical items, such as treatment tables, eyeglasses, lamps, etc.

Lab Coat- a coat-like covering for the upper body to protect against pigment splatter. Should be high necked and long sleeved.

Liquid Soap- the liquid form of soap. Usually more wasteful than other forms of soap.

Low Level Disinfectant- a disinfectant that kills most bacteria, fungi, and some viruses, but not tuberculosis or bacterial spores. Used for routine cleaning of non-critical items, such as floors, walls, blinds, etc.

Malaria- a very serious disease spread in tropical regions by mosquitos. The specific pathogen that causes the disease lives in the saliva of infected female mosquitos. When an infected female bites a human, the protozoa is transferred directly to the bloodstream, then to the liver, where it grows and multiplies.

Means of Transmission- the 4th link in the chain of infection, where an infectious agent finds a way to migrate to a Portal of Entry. This can be from a spill, a needle stick, or pigment splatter

Methicillin-Resistant Staphylococcus Aureus (MRSA)- a special type of staph infection which has developed a resistance to many antibiotics. Spread easily through contact between open skin and contaminated surfaces. Symptoms include inflammation, pus filled boils, bite-like lesions, and painful red bumps. MRSA must be treated by a healthcare professional.

Microorganism/Microbe- a microscopic organism. The word microbe is a shortened version that usually refers to pathogenic microorganisms

Mycobacterium Chelonae- a skin infection caused by harmful bacteria living in tap water used to dilute tattoo inks.

Needle Stick- an accidental puncture with a contaminated needle

Needle Stick Exposure Report- a detailed report written in the case of a needle stick. See the example in Chapter 6.

Non-Critical Items- everyday surfaces that may come in contact with intact skin. There are two categories of non-critcal items: clinical contact items and housekeeping items.

Non-Pathogenic Microorganisms- non harmful bacteria, viruses, fungi, or protozoa

Non-Reusable Items- items that must be thrown away, disposed of in a sharps container, or disposed of as regulated waste, such as pigment cups, used needles, and gauze.

Nosocomial/Hospital Acquired Infection- an infection contracted in a hospital, usually as a result of cross contamination by healthcare professionals.

Occupational Exposure- an incident where a person has been exposed to a dangerous substance while at work.

Occupational Safety and Health Administration (OSHA)- OSHA is the governing body responsible for protecting workers in the United States. OSHA creates laws to ensure safety in the workplace.

OPIM- Other Potentially Infectious Materials. Aside from blood, these materials pose a significant threat of infection to those who come in contact with them: Semen, vaginal secretions, cerebrospinal fluid (the clear fluid that surrounds your brain and spine), synovial fluid (a gooey liquid between your joints), pleural fluid (lung fluid),p ericardial fluid (the cushioning liquid that surrounds your heart), urine, peritoneal fluid (a lubricating fluid found in your stomach), vomit, amniotic fluid (fluid that surrounds and nourishes babies in pregnant women), saliva, any body fluid visibly contaminated with blood, all body fluids in situations where it is difficult or impossible to differentiate between body fluids, unfixed/detached organs

Opportunistic Infection- an infection that takes advantage of a body in a weakened state, such as an AIDS victim **Pathogenic Microorganisms/Pathogens**- harmful, disease causing bacteria, fungi, viruses, or protozoa.

Personal Protective Equipment (PPE)- Equipment/garments used to protect yourself from infectious agents in the workplace including pigment splatter. Includes labcoat, goggles, gloves, face mask, and closed toed shoes.

Pigment Splatter- this refers to permanent color or tattoo ink splattering during the procedure. Pigment/ink can splatter anywhere, and can cause infection via cross contamination as well as directly through contact with the eyes, nose, or mouth. If you get contaminated pigment into your eyes, nose, or mouth, flush the affected area with water for 15 minutes and seek medical attention.

Pigment Splatter Exposure Report- This is a detailed report of a pigment splatter incident. There is an example in Chapter 6.

Plain Soap- soap with no antimicrobial or antibacterial properties. Cleans only with the physical action of hand washing.

Portal of Entry- the 5th link in the chain of infection, the portal of entry is the doorway into a new host, such as a cut or mucous membrane (eyes, nose)

Portal of Exit- the 3rd link in the chain of infection, the portal of exit is an exit door from a reservoir, such as an open sink

Powdered Soap- abrasive powdered form of soap used to clean skin with friction as well as washing. Usually used to remove engine grease and difficult to clean surfaces, tough on hands.

Pre and Post Treatment Instructions- Instructions to be given to a body art client before the procedure to be informed of proper care, and to followed after the procedure.

Probiotic Bacteria- bacteria beneficial to the human digestive system

Prodromal Stage- the 2nd stage of infection, where a patient begins to feel sick, however symptoms have not yet fully developed into those unique to a specific disease

Protozoa- microscopic animals with the potential to cause disease
surfaces that require disinfection and sterilization (if possible)**Regulated Waste**- any kind of waste that is contaminated with enough OPIM to cause a hazard to the workplace. Contaminated laundry or disposables are considered regulated waste when you can squeeze a drop of blood from them.

Reservoir-the 2nd link in the chain of infection, a reservoir is a place an infectious agent lives in, such as a dirty implement

Reusable Items-items such as eyeglasses, autoclavable implements, treatment beds, and surfaces that require disinfection and sterilization (if possible)

Semi-Critical Items- items that may come in contact with open (non-intact) skin or mucous membranes such as the eyelids. Examples include tweezers, machine parts, etc. Use a high level disinfectant or sterilize, if possible.

Sepsis- infection, the state of being extremely dirty. This term can also refer to a deadly medical condition caused by the immune system's response to a severe infection. For the purposes of this book, the term sepsis is used to help understand the term asepsis, which refers to practicing healthcare in the cleanest way possible.

Sexually Transmitted Disease (STD)- a disease spread by sexual contact

Glossary

Sharps Container- a closable, leak-proof, puncture proof container labeled with the international biohazard symbol for the purpose of safe sharps disposal.

Spirilla- spiral-shaped bacteria

Spore-the offspring of a bacterium. Spores have a tough outer coat that only very high temperatures and/or pressure can destroy

Spore Strip- a biological indicator with a colored dot that changes color upon sterilization.

Staph Infection- an infection caused by cross contamination with the bacteria staphylococcus aureus. Symptoms may include red, inflamed skin, boils, and rashes, among others. If not treated, staph infections can develop severe and serious complications such as MRSA and blood poisoning

Staphylococcus Aureus- a bacteria found on the skin, S. aureus can become pathogenic if introduced into open skin (such as a fresh tattoo) and cause a staph infection.

Steam Autoclave- a sterilizer that uses hot steam and pressure to kill microorganisms.

Sterilization- the act of destroying all microorganisms on an item.

Sterilization Log- a record of implements sterilized. Shows when, how and other details of each sterilization cycle. Used to track proper sterilization of implements.

Sterilization Test Log- the certificate of compliance that comes from a sterilization monitoring/testing company after successful participation in the testing program.

Sterilizer Testing/Monitoring- the act of sending indicators to an outside company for monitoring sterilizer effectiveness. Recommended and in some cases required for body art professionals who sterilize.

Susceptible Host-this is the 6th link in the chain of infection, a susceptible host is a person or animal that falls victim to an infectious agent through the other links in the chain of infection.

Toxins- poisons released by pathogens that damage bodily functions.

Tuberculocidal- Tuberculosis killing

Tuberculosis- a bacterial infection of the lungs, transmitted through the air by an infected person's cough or sneeze

Used Implement Log- a log of needle size, lot number, expiration date, date used, artist who used the needle, and client who received work with that needle. Used to track implements in case of complications

Vaccination/Vaccine- also called immunization, a vaccine is a preventative injection of a weak version of a pathogen into the human body in order for the immune system to overcome that pathogen and develop antibodies for it.

Vector- any person, animal, insect, or object that acts as a carrier and spreads disease.

Virus- *the smallest* of the pathogens and the simplest microorganisms on earth. They contain a tiny core of genetic information, which is injected into a host in order to reproduce, usually this action causes disease.

Virucidal- virus killing

Viruses-pathogens that invade living cells in order to reproduce and cause infection

References

American Society for Microbiology (ASM). (2006). Microbial Spore Formation. Retrieved January 2012, from Microbe World: www.archives.microbeworld. org/

Bidartondo, M., & Read, D. (2008, August 17). Fungal specificity bottlenecks during orchid germination and development. Molecular Ecology , 3707-3716.

Bogitsh, B. J., Carter, C. E., & Oeltmann, T. N. (2013). Human Parasitology (4th Edition ed.). Waltham, MA, USA: Elsevier.

Boyd, R. (2006, September 20). Foam soap cuts down on environmental waste Retrieved April 2013, from Yale News: http://yaledailynews.com/

Centers for Disease Control and Prevention. (2014). Retrieved July 2014 from http:// www.cdc.gov/

Cottone, J. A., Terezhalmy, G. T., & Molinari, J. A. (1996). Practical Infection Control in Dentistry (2nd Edition ed.). Media, PA, USA: Williams & Wilkins.

Crow, S. R. (1989). Asepsis, The Right Touch: Something Old is Now New. Bossier City, Lousiana, USA: The Everett Companies.

Dietz, E., & Badavinac, R. (2002). Safety Standards and Infection Control for Dental Hygienists. Albany, NY, USA: Delmar.

Fuls, J. L., Rodgers, N. D., Fischler, G. E., Howard, J. M., Patel, M., Weidner, P. L., et al. (2008). Alternative Hand Contamination Technique To Compare the Activities of Antimicrobial and Nonantimicrobial Soaps under Different Test Conditions Applied and Environmental Microbiology , 74 (12), 3739-3744.

Getz, L. (2011, October). A Healthful Dose of Bacteria — Yogurt Is the Best Probiotic Source, but Clients Do Have Other Options. Today's Dietitian , 13 (10), p. 46.

Grice, E. A. (2008, 18-July). A Diversity Profile of the Human Skin Microbiota. Genome Research , 1043-1050.

Grice, E. A. (Performer). (2009 23-February). Diversity Profile of the Human Skin Microbiome in Health and Disease. Metagenomics, 2008, San Diego, CA, USA.

Health Canada. (2014). Nutrition. Retrieved January 2014 from http://www.hc-sc.gc.ca/

Infection Control Today (2014). Chemical Indicators. Retrieved June 2014 from http://www.infectioncontroltoday.com/articles/

Kalsi, J., Arya, M., Wilson, P., & Mundy, A. (2003). Hospital-acquired urinary tract infection. International Journal of Clinical Practice, 57 (5), 388-391.

Kampf, G., & Kramer, A. (2004). Epidemiologic Background of Hand Hygiene and Evaluation of the Most Important Agents for Scrubs and Rubs. Clinical Microbiology Reviews, 17 (4), 863-893.

Larson, E., Eke, P., Wilder, M., & Laughon, B. (1987). Quantity of soap as a variable in handwashing. Infection Control, 8 (9), 371-375.

Lea, A. S. (2013, June 25). Mycobacterium Chelonae. (B. A. Cunha, Ed.) Retrieved July 9, 2013, from Medscape Reference: http://emedicine.medscape.com/

Mayo Clinic. (2014) Retrieved February 2014 from http://www.mayoclinic.com/

Murphy, K. P. (2012). Janeway's Immunobiology (8th Edition ed.). New York, NY: Garland Science, Taylor and Francis Group, LLC.

OSHA. (1992, March 6). 1910.1030 Bloodborne Pathogens. Retrieved January 5, 2011, from Occupational Safety and Health Administration: https://www.osha gov/

Reese, R. E., & Douglas, R. G. (Eds.). (1983). A Practical Approach to Infectious Diseases. Boston, MA, USA: Little, Brown, and Company.

Seed, J. R. (1996). Protozoa: Pathogenesis and Defenses. In S. Baron (Ed.), Medical Microbiology (4th Edition ed.). Galveston, TX, USA: University of Texas Medical Branch.

Seedor, M. M. (1969). Introduction to Asepsis: A Programed Unit in Fundamentals of Nursing (2nd Edition ed.). New York: Teachers College, Columbia University.

References

Simon & Schuster Macmillan. (1995). Communicable Diseases. In Macmillan Health Encyclopedia (Vol. 2). New York, NY, USA: Simon & Schuster Macmillan.

Sompayrac, L. (2012). How the Immune System Works (4th Edition ed.). Chichester, West Sussex, UK: John Wiley and Sons, Ltd.

Songu, M., & Cingi, C. (2009). Sneeze reflex: facts and fiction. Therapeutic Advances in Respiratory Disease , 3, 131-141.

Southwick, F. S. (2003). Infectious Diseases in 30 Days. New York, NY, USA: McGraw Hill Companies.

Tims, S., van Wamel, W., Endtz, H. P., van Belkum, A., & Kayser, M. (2010). Microbial DNA fingerprinting of human fingerprints: dynamic colonization of fingertip microflora challenges human host inferences for forensic purposes International Journal of Legal Medicine, 124 (5), 477-481.

Todar, P. K. (2012). The Normal Bacterial Flora of Humans. Retrieved 2013 15-February from Todar's Online Textbook of Bacteriology: http: textbookofbacteriology.net/normalflora.html

Top, F. H., & Wehrle, P. F. (Eds.). (1976). Communicable and infectious diseases (8th Edition ed.). Saint Louis, MO, USA: The C. V. Mosby Company.

Turner, C., Jennison, M. W., & Edgerton, H. E. (1941). Public Health Applications of High-Speed Photography. American Journal of Public Health , 31, 319-324.

World Health Organization. (2014) Retrieved November 2013, from WHO: http:// www.who.int/

Index

Irene Kennerley is the senior research scientist for SofTap® Inc, an internationally renowned permanent cosmetics supplier offering the highest quality pigments, SofTap® patented 100% disposable hand tools, and professional education. Irene holds a bachelor of science in chemical engineering from San Jose State University and continues post-graduate studies independently. She also has many years of experience in the body art industry as a permanent cosmetic professional, beginning as an apprentice of Alexis Lawson, the founder of SofTap® Inc. Her combined knowledge of scientific principles and body art practice creates a valued voice to infection control in the body art workplace.

51921056R00122

Made in the USA
San Bernardino, CA
06 August 2017